Table of Contents

Start Programming with Alice

Jim Kelley

Version 2.4.1

START PROGRAMMING WITH ALICE

INTRODUCTION

After several years of using Alice to introduce programming in a college level first course in programming, I decided to put my notes on paper in a form that would serve as a text for the first six lessons of the course.

I have never attempted a writing of this magnitude since writing my Masters Thesis and the years made me loose sight of the scope of this undertaking. However, I stuck with it and this is my result. I hope all who use this in their classes or for their own self study, find it worthwhile.

As a user and proponent of Open Source Software, this book was written in its entirety using OpenOffice.org. I used Writer to convert it to a PDF for distribution.

FOR THE INSTRUCTOR:

One of the most frustrating parts of teaching computer related subjects is the books. There are many good books on many subjects. However, I find that for some courses I don't need 24 chapters on a topic that force my instruction into that chapter pattern or sequence. Often I would like a few chapters or even sections from a book, arranged in my sequence, and supplemented by my notes to create a lesson or part of a course.

The Alice textbooks available were few but for the most part quite good. But, I just needed a few basic lessons to allow me to introduce Computer Studies majors to the basic concepts of programming and objects before moving to Visual Basic. Also, I am fighting the tendency to teach the way I learned, with long laborious lectures on theory. I find that today's student suffers from what I call "The Sesame Street Syndrome". That is learning in 5 to 10 minute segments in an entertaining way. So, now we must adjust to the new paradigm of teaching and learning. I began this work in an attempt to match this learning pattern. Small segments of lessons with lots of hands on activities.

FOR THE STUDENT:

The goal for this book is to provide information on the Alice programming language in a concise, easy to read format. Lots of hands-on work, lots of examples and some quizzes to highlight some of the important point of the lesson. Remember, you do not learn to program by reading about it. Programming is learned by doing. Do lots of examples, invent projects on your own. It takes years to become a good programmer and if that is your goal, you need to practice. Think back to times you learned anything, riding a bike, shooting a basketball, playing soccer, playing an instrument, all came about with lots of practice. So, dive into the book and start producing lots of Alice movies.

SUPPLEMENTS:

It is my intention to supplement this book with a web page. This way I can provide updates to the material on a moments notice. We are teaching in a field where change is good, frequent and where printed copy does not stand the test of time. Test banks while nice, often leave the instructor explaining why a question was wrong. Sometimes I have found that I agree with the student and have no rationale as to why the test bank had a different answer. So, don't expect big fancy test banks. Perhaps some questions that I use in my classes but in a format the instructor can modify to their own satisfaction. Programming Exercises as I come up with new material would be included in a supplemental web page. Once again, use what you like or make your own. PowerPoint slides, why? Students usually sleep through them and then want to print them out. However, there is a HUGE demand for PowerPoint slides to match the Chapters so keep looking to my web site for my slides. I will be using Apache OpenOffice to create these slides. Look on my web site for some short lessons where I used Alice to illustrate a basic concept. You may also use CamStudio or Jing (for free) to create short lessons. Use YouTube and make an Alice movie and post it to make a point.

SUMMARY

I am a computer programmer who turned teacher. I see a need in my own classroom for a text with lots of examples that take a student through creating Alice movies, step by step. Hands on is the way to learn programming and this text is designed to facilitate the students hands on experience. This text gives the theory in text for reference or reading, then examples written to lead a student through practicing the theory with step by step examples. So, here is my attempt to teach Alice Programming, Step-by-Step.

Alice 2.3/2.4 Programming Language
Alice Overview

Objectives:

- Describe the concept of the Alice Programming Language
- Explain how to obtain and install Alice
- Use the Alice Tutorials

Lesson 0.0 - Overview of Alice

Alice Versions 2.2, 2.3 and Alice 2.4, versions of Alice programming software that will put you into the world of 3-D animation. The surprise is how quickly one can master the art of creating animated movies or 3-D games. Developed by Carnegie Mellon University by faculty like Randy Pausch, Wanda Dann and Steven Cooper. It was named after Lewis Carroll's book, "Alice in Wonderland" and reflects Mr. Carroll's mathematical background.

Finally, a programming language that is simple and above all FUN! Alice was developed for the beginning programmer. Alice is used at both the high school and university level. It was designed to get young people, particularly young women, interested in programming. It is also a great way to start to master the skills of 3-D programming for a future in creating virtual reality, animated movies, special effects in movies and those ever popular computer games.

Why study Alice? Alice is not a "real world" programming language. Applications are not and never will be written in Alice. Then, what is the purpose of Alice? Alice was designed to teach the principles of programming without the encumbrance of syntax error. Plus, it was designed to be fun and learning is always supposed to be fun. Results may not be Halo or Hollywood, but with a little effort the beginner can show off some pretty amazing 3-D virtual worlds.

In Alice, the programmer creates a world and then populates the world with various objects. If the movie takes place in the city, one would populate the world with buildings, streets, signs, etc . The programmer can animate many of these objects and make them perform various actions that would be done by a similar object in the 'real world'. For example: make a soldier march, a skater skate across the pond and twirl and jump, a car move down the highway, a space ship take off and many other actions for various objects.

Learn to use Alice by telling a story. Compose a short story and then tell this story using Alice. There are examples of teachers using Alice to illustrate their courses. Alice can be used to teach a language, teach a math problem, used in science and physics. The potential is endless. For some examples of how Alice has been used there are some programs on YouTube and on other Alice related web sites.

Lesson 0.1 – How To Get Alice

Another great feature of Alice is that it is FREE. Yes, it can be downloaded from www.alice.org at no cost. Once the Alice zip file is downloaded, it must be unzipped. It will create an Alice folder with a sub folder named "Required" and two executable files, Alice.exe and SlowandSteadyAlice.exe.

To execute Alice, first try the Alice.exe and if that works on the computer in use, stick with that one. It may take a while to load since there are a lot of graphics to load. If it is to be run on an older computer, try SlowandSteadyAlice.exe.

To download and install Alice:

Go to the Alice website http://www.alice.org and download Alice 2.4, (or one of the older versions like 2.3 or Alice 2.2) to the computer. Unzip the file and it will put two files and a sub folder on the computer.

Alice.exe

SlowandSteadyAlice.exe

A sub folder named "Required"

Click on the Alice.exe to execute the Alice program

Figure 0.1.1 – Alice.org web site

A tip for those who work on many different machines. Since Alice does not place any code in the operating system or make any registry changes, it is completely standalone. Once it has been unzipped, the files can be moved from computer to computer without any installation. Alice can be loaded to a "Flash Drive", "USB Drive", "Memory Stick", "SD", etc.. It does take up quite a bit of room so make sure there is enough room to install. This way there is access to Alice wherever it is needed. NOTE: The "Required" folder and all of its contents must be in the same folder as the .exe file for Alice.

It is also worthy to note that Alice is available for Windows, Linux and MAC OS operating systems.

Alice is under continuous development. Currently there are two versions available. Alice 2.4, and Alice 3.0. There are also downloads for "Older Versions". We will cover the 2.3 and 2.4 versions in this book.

Lesson 0.2 – Welcome to Alice! Dialog Box

The Welcome to Alice 2.4 dialog box contains six tabs. This lesson gives a brief explanation of each tab. This dialog box appears when Alice first opens. If you need to bring up this dialog box after it has closed, there are several ways. First, from the File menu you can select either "New World" or "Open World". Then, from the Help menu you can select "Tutorials" or "Example Worlds". Any of these four selections will open the dialog box. The Tutorials give an excellent overview of the capabilities of Alice and is recommended as a starting place for all students.

The Examples are another great place for a student to see the capabilities of Alice and a good reference for seeing code or animations to assist in completing original worlds.

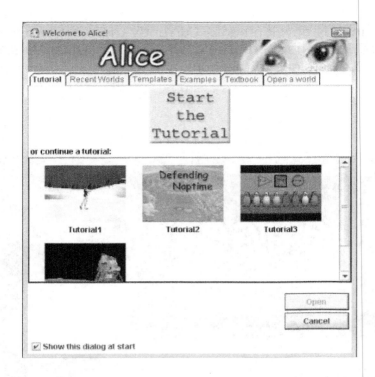

Tab 1 – Tutorial – There are 4 different tutorials which go over the basics of Alice programming.

Tab 2 – Recent Worlds – This page shows all of your recent work for easy access.

Tab 3 – Templates – Six different templates for different types of worlds.

Tab 4 – Example – Six different examples of Alice Programs.

Tab 5 – Textbook – Alice programs that correspond to the official Alice Text book.

Tab 6 – Open A World – Allows the user to browse for a file, select the file and open it.

SECTION 1

Alice Programming Theory

This section describes the Alice Programming Environment. How to use the Alice Integrated Development Environment (IDE) and how to write code for Alice programs. There are seven (7) chapters in this section.

1. Alice Basics
2. Alice Programming
3. Decisions
4. Repetition
5. Methods
6. Functions
7. Events
8. Classes

Chapter 1 – Alice Basics

Objectives:

- Explain the Alice environment.
- Describe Properties and Methods of Objects.
- Use the Quad view.
- Storyboard an Alice Program.

Lesson 1.0 The Alice Environment

When the Alice programming environment is started, it is necessary to be familiar with the different areas of the screen, the purpose of these areas and how we will refer to each of them.

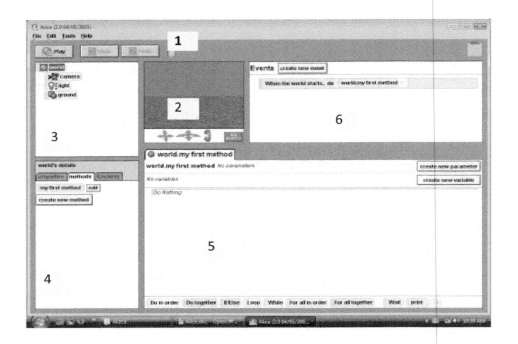

Figure 1.0.1

Each area of the Alice Environment can be defined as follows:

Toolbar(1): Contains a Play Button that plays a virtual world. An Undo Button which will undo the previous operation. A Redo button that reverses the last Undo. A trash can for deleted objects. It can also contain one or more clipboards to temporarily store objects.

World View Window(2): Shows a view of a virtual world. Each virtual world has a camera and the window acts as the viewfinder for this camera. It has three controls that allows the camera to move and rotate, the controls are at the bottom of the window.

Object Tree(3): Contains a list of all of the object for the virtual world. Each object has a name and it is listed on the object tree. Use this panel to select the appropriate object when the details panel is used.

Details Panel(4): Shows detailed information about an object that has been selected in the World View window or in the Object Tree. There are three (3) tabs in this panel. The Properties tab contains the attributes that describe the object selected. The Methods tab contains the methods or things that the object can do. The functions tab contains the functions (subprograms) associated with the object selected.

Method Editor(5): This is where the programmer creates methods which are simply, a set of instructions that causes some action to take place.

Events Editor(6): Events happen as the world plays. It may be a key pressed or a mouse button clicked or a number of other predetermined events. Alice responds to a these events by triggering a program sequence.

In Review:

1.0.1 The _____ _____ is where the programmer creates methods.

1.0.2 There are three tabs in the Details Panel:
(1)_____(2)_____(3)_____

1.0.3 Each virtual world has a camera and the _____ _____ _____ acts as the viewfinder for this camera.

1.0.4 You may have more than one clipboard to temporarily store objects. (True / False)

1.0.5 Alice responds to _____ by triggering a program sequence.

Lesson 1.1 Alice Tutorials

Alice comes complete with four(4) excellent tutorials to help the programmer get started. The first time Alice is loaded, the tutorial dialog box should appear. If it does not appear go to the menu bar and select Help, then Tutorials. Completing these tutorials will familiarize the user with the basics of Alice programming.

At this point, I recommend the first two tutorials are completed before moving to the next step. If there are problems with the tutorials repeat them until a comfort level with their content has bee achieved. Going through all of the tutorials is important, but going through these two tutorials carefully will get the user started. Understanding the concepts in these tutorials will help do the exercises in future lessons.

The four standard tutorials are:

- Skater
- Defending Naptime
- Penguins
- Space

Tutorial 1 – Skater covers the basics of the IDE. Then it goes into creating a basic Alice movie. This, and the other tutorials allow you to practice using Alice by leading you through the keystrokes and mouse clicks to create a project.

Tutorial 2 – Defending Naptime tells a short story. It demonstrates dialog bubbles, sound and how to create a new method.

Tutorial 3 – Penguins demonstrates how to make an Alice world respond to mouse clicks and key presses.

Tutorial 4 – Space World show how to create scenes, select worlds and add new objects.

Figure 1.1.1 – Alice Tutorials Dialog Box

Doing all of these tutorials will help the user gain an understanding of the power of the Alice Programming Language. These are more than silly little movies. They encompass all of the principles of all programming languages in a fun, easy to use programming environment that does much to prevent the new programmer from making many programming errors.

In Review:

1.1.1 Alice comes with _____ tutorials.

1.1.2 You can access the tutorials by clicking on the _____ menu and then
_____

1.1.3 The tutorials are designed to present only the advanced Alice commands.
(True / False)

Lesson 1.2 Properties & Methods of Objects

Each object has associated properties, methods and functions. To view these, select the object to be worked with. Make the selection in the "Object Tree". Note that there are selections for the "World", the "Camera" and "Light". These are also objects that can be manipulated in the code. Some objects have a + sign next to them. This means the object is a composition of several other objects that can also be manipulated separately.

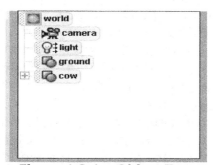

Figure 1.2.1 – Object Tree

Each object in an Alice world has properties. These are simply values that describe the object's characteristics. As an object is placed in the Alice world, its properties can be changed. The object's color may be changed, for instance. The object's property values may be changed as the program executes.

Figure 1.2.2 – Details Panel

Objects are capable of doing things. The things an object can do are called methods. One of the methods is the "say" method. This allows the object to "say" things. Some methods can move the object up, down, left, right. The methods quite often are things that object could do in real life. The penguin object can move and walk, a plane object can move but I doubt if the designer gave it the ability to walk. Methods are consistent with the object's capabilities in the real world.

Objects can become very complicated because, quite often, objects are made from other objects or groups of objects. As the user learns to use Alice they will manipulate an object and find the object coming apart. An example may be one of the people objects. These are composite objects. The head can move, the arms can move, the legs can move and it is necessary to manipulate the methods of these objects, coordinate each part of the object so simulated activities that that object needs to do in the course of the movie are realistic.

It is important to recognize that the Alice Gallery is NOT a gallery of objects. It is a gallery of classes. What is the difference? The best way to look at a class is to compare it to a recipe. It is a recipe to create what is called an object. This recipe may gather several objects to present them as an object in a virtual world. So, when several of the same object are placed in the world in use, the recipe to create the class is used to create multiple instances of the same class. Each instance is a completely separate object.

In Review:

1.2.1 Each object has associated _____, _____ and _____.

1.2.2 The things objects can do are called _____.

1.2.3 _____ are values that describe the object's characteristics.

1.2.4 The best way to look at a class is to compare it to a _____.

1.2.5 Quite often, _____ are made from other _____ or groups of _____.

18

Lesson 1.3 Try This

Now it is time to create an Alice movie from scratch:

1. Select File > New World from top menu bar.
2. Select the "Water" world.
3. Click on the GREEN "Add Objects" button in the world area.
4. Now, at the bottom of the screen there is the "Gallery" of objects that can be used in the world. Go to the end of the gallery icon bar and select the one titled Create 3-D Text
5. There is a dialog box that contains a text box with "The quick brown fox" in the box. Change this text to Your first and last names
6. Click on the OK button at the bottom of the dialog box.
7. Click on the Done button. A GREEN button on the right side just above the gallery.
8. Now Click on the "PLAY" button (upper left) to play your first movie.
9. You are now an Alice programmer

Lesson 1.4 Quad View

As multiple objects are placed on the world, it is often difficult to get them lined up in proper starting positions, orient them to various other objects on the stage, etc.. As objects are added to the world, in the upper right corner of the screen there are radio buttons for single view and quad view. Quad view will allow a view of the 3-D objects from the top, front and side.

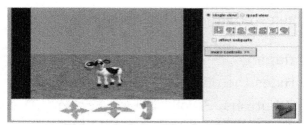

Figure 1.4.1 – Single View.

Figure 1.4.2 – Quad View.

19

Next, the Layout Tools found in the upper right corner of the screen. There is a description of each tool that can be seen by moving the mouse pointer over the tool. There are 7 different tools and the best way to learn what they do is to place an object on a world and experiment with each of these tools.

The seven tools are:

1. Move objects freely
2. Move objects up and down
3. Turn objects left and right with mouse
4. Turn objects forward and backwards with mouse
5. Tumble objects with the mouse
6. Resize objects with the mouse
7. Copy objects with the mouse

Using single view and quad view these tools help position and size objects on the stage. Then, as the movie progresses, the objects will perform correctly on the screen.

There is also a button labeled "more controls" in this area. This contains some advanced functions not covered by this text. Pressing the button reveals six additional controls:

- Aspect Ratio: width versus height of windows. Default is 4/3, selected from a drop down.
- Lens Angle slider control: Moves the camera lense
- Drop dummy at camera: Create a new dummy object at the current position of the camera.
- Drop dummy at selected object: Creates a new dummy object at the current selected object.
- Move camera to dummy
- Fewer Controls: Hides the advanced controls.

There are two additional buttons, Scroll View and Zoom. These are used to assist you in positioning the objects when you are in quad view. Below the right two panels of quad view have been enlarged using the zoom feature. The Zoom and the Scroll View are mouse controls.

Figure 1.4.3

I encourage the new user to learn how to use this view and the various other positioning tools found in this area of the editor.

In Review:

1.4.1 Quad view will allow a view of the 3-D objects from the _____, _____ and _____.

1.4.2 There are two additional buttons, _____ and _____. These are used to assist you in positioning the objects when you are in quad view.

1.4.3 The _____ Tools found in the upper right corner of the screen.

1.4.4 There are _____ different Layout tools

Lesson 1.5 Storyboarding

First, there must be an idea for a story. The next step is to put that story on paper and get it in a logical order. It could be viewed as a road map to lead the programmer through the story to insure steps are not missed. This is called "storyboarding" the movie. The concept comes from advertising agencies where it is used for developing scripts for TV advertisements, Learning to use this tool will help make better movies and cut down on development time.

A storyboard can be elaborate or just a group of simple sketch drawings of the movie in development. It is not necessary for it to be a work of art. Stick figures, shapes, lines are okay, it just needs to assist in the organization of ideas and the flow of the movie. It usually includes the script for the movie if there is interaction, talking and/or music included.

The first step in developing a storyboard is to develop a script for the movie. A written plan for the entire movie. The objects to be used and what part the object will play in the movie. Then, take this script and draw a rough series of pictures showing what the stage will look like at various points in the movie, this is the storyboard.

Then, review the storyboard to insure all of the main elements have been included and pay special attention to the order of activities. This is where the order of events are reviewed closely to make sure the movie flows correctly from beginning to end. It is not uncommon to make significant changes here. Remember "Weeks of programming can save hours of planning".

Yes, the movie could be developed without taking the time to do this step, however, that only works for short clips and they are usually not well organized and often a disappointment to the developer once they are finished. Then the developer is left with the decision to live with it or spend more time in fixing the movie. Just like any other programming project, an Alice program should be carefully planned.

The storyboard does not have to be fancy. My example is just some stick figures and comments to illustrate what is to be done in the movie and in what sequence.

21

Another approach is to draw each screen on a post-it, 3 x 5 card, or sheet of paper. This allows you to re-arrange sequence or substitute a new drawing for the screen. Let's look at a simple example.

SAMPLE SCRIPT:
1. Place 3 characters on the screen
2. First character jumps up and down three times
3. Second character turns around five times.
4. Third character moves forward one meter then back one meter.

SAMPLE STORYBOARD:

This is just a quick, crude example of a storyboard for a simple movie. No fancy artistry. It is not really necessary for such a short movie but would be a great planning tool for a longer movie. Remember, all of those great advertisements you see on television began on a storyboard.

In Review:

1.5.1 A _____ could be viewed as a road map to lead the programmer through a story.

1.5.2 The first step in developing a storyboard is to develop a _____ for the movie.

1.5.3 A storyboard can consist of some simple drawings for each frame.   (True / False)

Lesson 1.6 Pseudocode

Another method of making sure you stay on track with your movie is to outline your story line in what is called pseudocode. Pseudocode is nothing more than an outline. A list of statements that tell you, step-by-Step how to construct your movie. This may also be your preferred method of organizing your thoughts when you move to another programming language. Looking back at our storyboard example the pseudocode is nothing more than the sample script:

PSEUDOCODE:

1. Place 3 characters on the screen
2. First character jumps up and down three times
3. Second character turns around five times
4. Third character moves forward one meter then back one meter.

While not as effective as storyboarding your movie, pseudocode is second best. In any case, you need to plan your movie to keep it on track. This is especially important when you begin to produce more complex movies with several scenes, added methods and events. When the story line gets complex, some method of planning must be used or your movie will fall short of its original intent.

In Review:

1.6.1 Pseudocode is nothing more than an _____.

1.6.2 You may also use pseudocode when _____.

1.6.3 _____ or _____ may be used to plan your movie.

Lesson 1.7 Summary

We covered a lot of material in this chapter. First, we identified the various windows of the Alice IDE. Next, a look at the tutorials. Each one shows some important aspect of creating an Alice movie. Then a discussion of Properties, Methods and Functions of objects. Quad View helps in positioning objects on the stage. The layout controls move the objects, as well as make copies of them, if needed. The chapter also introduces some other tools to assist in making your objects move about the screen.

Lastly, we took a look at the concept of a storyboard. A planning tool to help the programmer get all the action in the correct order. This is important in Alice and every other programming language. The saying "Failing to Plan is a Plan to Fail" is just as important in programming as it is in life.

Chapter 2 - Alice Programming

Objectives

- Use 3D objects.
- Describe how to create and use variables
- Explain how to use all of the data types.
- Describe object properties, methods and functions.

Lesson 2.0 - Overview of 3-D and Object Movement

Alice is a 3-D world and that just makes programming more interesting. It is important to start thinking about front, back, left, right, top and bottom. This can make some things just a little more tricky but with a little practice it can be mastered. Many of the objects can move forward, backwards, left, right, up and down, this is referred to as the six degrees of freedom.

Each object has a center, the trick here is that it may not be the exact center of the bounding box for the particular object. Select an object and then click on the Properties tab in the Details area and scroll down to the pointOfView entry and click the blue box to the right, there will be three numbers. (distance to the left of center, distance above center, distance forward of center) This translates to the distance of the center of the object from the center of the world. Negative figures may indicate the object is below the ground.

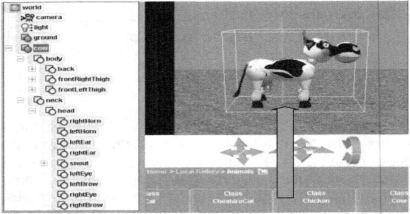

Figure 2.0.1 – The Cow Object

Figure 2.0.1 shows the cow object. The arrow points to the intersect of three lines (one green, one red and one blue) that indicate the center of this object. When manipulating this object this is the center of the object and the motion. Also, note in the Object Tree all of the components of this object that can be manipulated. Remember, these sub objects also have centers that affect their movement.

Now, let's move our objects using methods. Methods are defined as things an object can do and if there is an object that can move it should have a method that allows it to move. Using the object tree, select an object in the world, then select the Methods tab in the Details area to see all those things that the object can do. If an animate object is selected, there should be a method named move. If this is dragged to the Editor area and dropped over the words "Do Nothing". A menu will pop up that asks for direction and how far to move. Answer these questions, play the movie and watch the object move.

Look at some of the other methods for the object. Such methods as "turn to face", "point at", "stand up" are listed. To really understand the full capabilities of Alice it is necessary to play with these methods to learn what the object can do with just a point and a click. Remember, not all objects will share the same methods.

In Review:

2.0.1 In Alice 3D programming it is important to start thinking about _____, _____, _____, _____, _____ and _____.

2.0.2 _____ are defined as things an object can do.

2.0.3 Many of the objects can move forward, backwards, left, right, up and down, this is referred to as the _____.

2.0.4 All objects will share the same methods. (True / False)

2.0.5 Select the Methods tab in the _____ area to see all those things that the object can do.

Lesson 2.1 - Placing Objects in the World

Once we have selected a world template (grass, dirt, snow, sand, etc.), we need to place some objects in the world. To do this we need to select the green button in the lower right corner of the World View that is labeled "Add Objects".

Figure 2.1.1 Add Objects button

We then move to the Add Objects screen (see figure 2.1.2). Here is where we can add new objects to the world, manipulate those objects into poses, move them around the world, and other set up tasks. There is a larger area to view the world and a choice of viewing your world in a single screen or in a "quad" view that shows the world from the front, right side, and top. This tool can be used to orient objects more precisely.

Figure 2.1.2 Add Objects Single View

Figure 2.1.3 Add Objects Quad View

There are two ways to add an object to the world. First way to click on the class then click on the Add object button as shown. (see figure 2.1.4)

Figure 2.1.4 Click to Add Object

The second way is to drag-and-drop the class on the screen in the place you want to put the object. (see figure x.x)

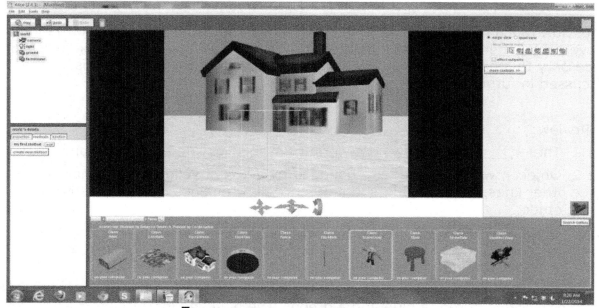
Figure 2.1.5 Drag-and-drop Object

If you look carefully at Figure 2.1.5 you will see a yellow 3-D box with a Green Vertical Line, a red line and a blue line off the bottom of the green line. The green line represents up and down for that object, the red line represents how the direction the object will move left and right and the blue line represents how the object will move forward and backward. These are important when programming your objects to move about the screen.

Try This:
1. Select the grass world and click on the "Add Objects" button
2. Select the Animals Gallery and find the "Bunny" object and place on the grass
3. Again, from the Animals Gallery, select the "Penguin" object and place on the grass
4. Place the two objects side by side facing the camera.
5. Click on the "Done" button
6. Select the "bunny" object and click on the method tab and select the method that makes the bunny "move" forward 5 meters, drag and drop it on the methods editor pane.
7. Select the "penguin" object and click on the method tab and select the method that makes the penguin "walk" forward 5 meters, drag and drop it on the methods editor pane.
8. PLAY

Note how much more realistic the penguin movement is as compared to the bunny movement. There is no "walk" method for the bunny. To simulate walking it is necessary to create that capability as a new method for the bunny. This will be discussed in future lessons.

In Review:

2.1.1 The _____ view shows the world from the front, left side and top.

2.1.2 Objects, when selected are bounded by a box of yellow lines. There are also three other lines, a red, a blue and a green. All three lines intersect at the _____ of the object.

2.1.3 Objects, when selected are bounded by a box of yellow lines. There are also three other lines, a red, a blue and a green. The green line indicates the _____ and _____ direction for that object.

2.1.3 Objects, when selected are bounded by a box of yellow lines. There are also three other lines, a red, a blue and a green. The blue line indicates the _____ and _____ direction for that object.

2.1.3 Objects, when selected are bounded by a box of yellow lines. There are also three other lines, a red, a blue and a green. The red line indicates the _____ and _____ direction for that object.

Lesson 2.2 – Using Primitive Methods to Position Objects

Another way to position objects when in Add Object Mode, is to use the primitive methods. If the object is selected in the "Object Tree" you can "right click" on the object name and a drop down list of primitive methods will appear and a method can then be selected to position the object.

The "Lunar Lander" needs to be turned ¼ revolution. The example 2.2.1 shows the Lander selected in the object tree with the available selections to accomplish this task shown in the drop down menus.

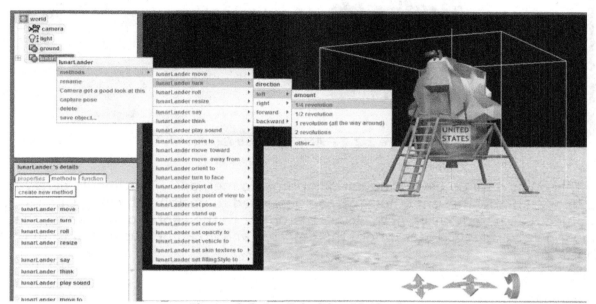

Figure 2.2.1 – Primitive Methods

The first drop down, select "methods", the next drop down shows the methods, select "lunarLander turn", next drop down shows directions, choose "left", the last choice is the amount the object should turn, here select "1/4 revolution". Press enter and the object will turn ¼ revolution to the left.

The next figure (Figure 2.2.2) shows the position of the Lander after the enter key is pressed and the turn method is completed.

29

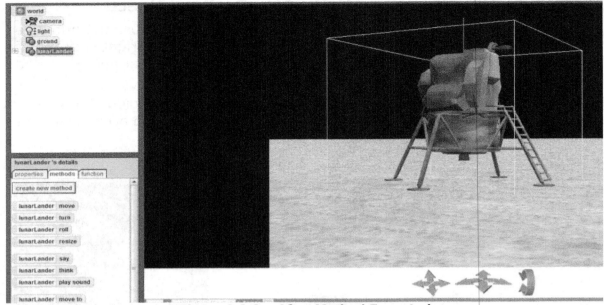

Figure 2.2.2 – After Method Executed

Try this on several objects using various primitive methods. This should give you a good idea on how these methods can be best used to position objects. One use is if an object is created out of view. Move the object to the center of the world, this should give you a good idea where the object is and it can be positioned from that point.

In Review:

2.2.1 You may use the _____ methods to position objects in the "Add Object" screen.

2.2.2 To access the primitive methods for an object, _____ on the selected object in the _____.

Lesson 2.3 - Variables

Variables are vital elements in every programming language. A portion of memory that can be used to store a piece of information. In a program a variable is created to store some information and is given a name so the programmer can use the data in various processing instructions. The contents of the variable can be used in calculations, used for display, changed, by various program instructions.

So, a variable is a storage place for numbers, strings, objects and others. It stores these objects so they can be used in the processing of the program.

As in other programming languages there are four categories of variables:

Local Variables   This belongs to a specific Method and can only be used by instructions that pertain to that method.

Parameter Variables   Used to hold an argument that is passed to a method when it is called.

Class-Level Variables   Like a property that belongs to a specific object and all instances of that object.

World-Level Variables   Like a property that belongs to the world.

Each variable must have a name created using the following rules:

- Must be unique within its scope (local, world, class, parameter).
- Name should be meaningful.
- Use the camelCase convention.

Types of variables includes:

Number   Holds numbers, any number.

Boolean   Holds either True or False

Object   Holds an object

Other   More specific types like: strings, sound, color and others.

Once a variable, has been created an initial value must be established.

Steps to create a variable:

1. In the Method Editor, click on the ***create new variable*** button.
2. In the ***Create New Local Variable*** dialog box, enter the name of the variable.
3. Select a data type.
4. Enter an initial value.
5. Click on **OK** button.
6. A tile for the variable should appear in the Method Editor's variable area.

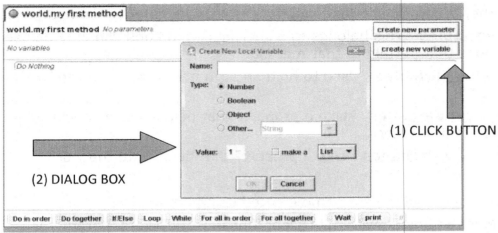

Figure 2.3.1 – Creating a Variable

To assign a value to a variable, give the variable an initial value when it is created. In the course of running the program it may be changed depending on conditions

1. Drag the variable tile to the Methods Editor.
2. In the menu select **Set Value**
3. Select a value from the list or other to type a new value.

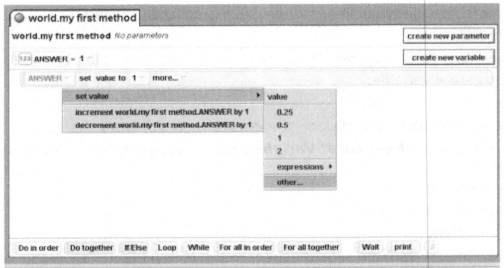

Figure 2.3.2 – Setting a Variable

Remember a variable must be initialized to a value. If the value is not in the list choose other... and a calculator will pop up and you can specify the value you need. While variables have an initial value, the value can be changed in the running of the program. The variable is a storage place for a value that can be used or changed in the running of the program.

32

In Review:

2.3.1 A _____ is a portion of memory that can be used to store a piece of information.

2.3.2 Once a variable, has been created an initial value must be established. (True / False)

2.3.3 There are _____ categories of variables.

2.3.4 Types of variables include: _____, _____, _____, _____ .

Lesson 2.4 - Alice Properties, Methods and Functions.

When using Alice, the mouse is used to select commands. Then watch what happens on the screen. If the skater ends up in the wrong place or skates in the wrong direction, just go back and change the command. Alice is mainly a drag and drop programming language. One of the major benefits of the language is that the beginning programmer does not have to be concerned with syntax errors. No matter what instructions are used, the syntax will not cause compile errors. The program may do weird things but it will run. It supports all three programming structures: sequence, decision and repetition.

Working with Alice, the user will not experience the most difficult part of writing computer programs – writing all of the detailed instructions, in precisely the correct language and syntax, for every little thing that is going to happen on the screen. This is the big "turn-off" for beginner programmers. They often are frustrated in trying to figure out what they did so wrong to cause the program not to run as expected.

The programmer can change the values of variables and of properties of objects as the program is running. The previous lesson established how to set the value of a variable. Now, review the steps to change the value of a property of an object:

1. Select the object with the property to be changed.
2. Drag the property's tile from the Details Panel into the Methods Editor.
3. Drop the tile, a menu will appear allowing selection of a value for the property.

Using Functions

A function is a special type of method that completes a task with the given parameters (if any required) and returns a result to the program that called the function.

1. Select the object
2. Select the functions tab in the Details Panel to display a list of tiles that represent the object's functions

A function might be used to measure how close an object is to another object, do a math operation, create a random number, interact with the user, and many other operations. Look at the functions for the World, the Camera, a person object, a building object, a vehicle object, to get an idea of the wide variety of objects available.

Getting Input from the User

The world object has three primitive functions that can be used to ask the user to input a value. Select the world object and then scroll down in its list of functions there is a "ask user" category. the three choices are:

- ask user for a number
- ask user for yes or no
- ask user for a string

When one of these options are selected a dialog box is displayed that will accept either a number, a yes or no or a string value. The ask user functions are used to set a value of a function as part of the set value of a variable. Rather than the program selecting a specified value, the user has an opportunity through the dialog box to set that value.

Math Expressions

Most programs require calculations in their course of execution. Alice programmers can do addition, subtraction, multiplication and division. Math is implemented using the "set value to" instruction. The programmer simply selects expressions rather than a value and then enters the mathematical expression that assigns the appropriate value to the variable.

Strings and Text

A string is defined as a sequence of one or more characters. Alice has a full range of features for working with strings and text. Strings are entered in one of three different ways:

1. When you create a string variable.
2. When you *set value* for a string variable.
3. Some objects have a "Say" value which requires a string.

There will be times that it is necessary to combine two strings to display a result of some action. This could be asking the user to enter their name so the character object can say, "Hi Elmo" or whatever name was entered.

This is accomplished in the "Say" method for objects that have the say method in their methods list. Select the Say method, enter the string "Hi" then after the "joined with" select the variable that contains the name that the user entered

We can also have an object "Say" a numeric value by using the numeric variable name with the "as a string" modifier.

In Review:

2.4.1 When using Alice, the _____ is used to select commands.

2.4.2 The most difficult part of writing computer programs – writing all of the detailed instructions, in precisely the correct language and _____.

2.4.3 A _____ is a special type of method that completes a task with the given parameters (if any required) and returns a result to the program that called the function.

2.4.4 The _____ _____ has three primitive functions that can be used to ask the user to input a value.

2.4.5 A _____ is defined as a sequence of one or more characters.

Lesson 2.5 – Do Together / Do In Order

When it is necessary that two or more objects move at the same time the "Do Together" structure is used. The Do Together structure makes all of the instructions contained within the structure execute at the same time. This allows the programmer to make several things happen simultaneously.

A good example of using Do Together is shown below. The car and the driver are two objects that need to move together at the same time, same rate, same distance and same distance.

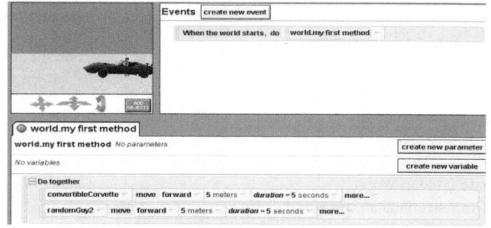

Figure 2.5.1

The car object and the randomGuy object move forward simultaneously, the same distance at the same speed. If those instructions were not in the Do Together

35

structure, the car would move then the driver would move and this would not look like the guy was driving the car.

The Do in Order structure is a way to group instructions that should happen in a specific order. This is used when the programmer needs to insure that a group of instructions are processed in an exact order. The Do in Order structure is implied in a program but there are situations where this structure needs to be nested in another structure to achieve the desired actions.

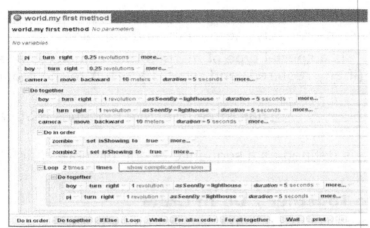

Figure 2.5.2

In our example in Figure 2.5.2, the two boys run around the lighthouse together but the two zombies appear on the screen one at a time even though they are inside the "Do Together" structure.

In Review:

2.5.1 When it is necessary that two or more objects move at the same time the _____ _____ structure is used.

2.5.2 The Do in Order structure is a way to group instructions that should happen in a _____ _____.

2.5.3 The ____ _____ structure allows the programmer to make several things happen simultaneously.

Lesson 2.6 – Try This.

1. Create a Moon World
2. Put an Astronaut on the world
3. Create 3 variables (num1 = 1; num2 = 1; answer = 1)
4. Drag variable num1 to the method area and set value to 1
5. replace the 1 with the world function "***ask user for a number***"

6. choose the other option "**Enter a Number:**"

7. Drag variable num2 to the method area and set value to 1

8. Repeat steps 5 & 6

9. Drag the variable answer to the method area and set value to 1

10.   Drag the num1 variable to replace the value 1.

11.   Click on the arrow next to num1 and choose math

12.   Choose option *num1+*

13.   Choose expression and num2

14.   Have the Astronaut say "**The answer is** "

15.   go to world functions and select ***a joined with b*** and drop over the text "The answer is".

16.   Select other and enter "**x**"

17.   Replace the **x** with the world function ***what as a string***

18.   Select expressions and num2.

19.   Run the project and respond to each request for a number with the number 2

20.   The astronaut should answer "The answer is 4.0".

```
world.my first method ( )
num1 = 1 , num2 = 1 , answer = 1

    num1 set value to ( ask user for a number question = Enter a Number: )

    num2 set value to ( ask user for a number question = Enter a Number: )

    answer set value to ( ( num1 + num2 ) )

    astronaut say ( The Answer is joined with ( answer as a string ) )
```

Chapter 3 – Decisions

Objectives

- Use the decision structures.
- Use the billboard object
- Create 3D text

Lesson 3.1 - Decisions

The Decision Structure programmatically evaluates expressions and based on the outcome, decide which code to execute. The expression evaluated must evaluate to a "Boolean" value or in more simple terms an expression that evaluates to either "True" or "False".

At the bottom of the Method Editor there is a group of tiles and one of these tiles is titled "If/Else". To use the decision structure drag this tile to the appropriate place in the Method editor of the program. This will result in a If Else structure placed in your program. The line after the If statement, is a box for the true statements, next line is the Else and the fourth line is for the False statements. Put the statement or statements to be executed in the True side for those to be executed if the evaluation of the expression results in true. Put the statements to be executed if the expression is evaluated as false in the false side after the else statement. If the false side does not contain any instructions this is a single sided decision structure that only executes alternate instructions if the expression evaluates to true.

Constructing a "Boolean" Expression for Evaluation

There are six (6) relational operators:

1. == Equal to
2. != Not Equal to
3. >= Greater than or equal to
4. <= Less than or equal to
5. > Greater than
6. < Less than

Use these to compare two values or the contents of two variables or the content of a variable and a value. Based on the comparison of the two, the relational operator selected gives a result of True or False. This determines which code gets executed. When the appropriate code completes, the program continues with the next instruction after the decision structure.

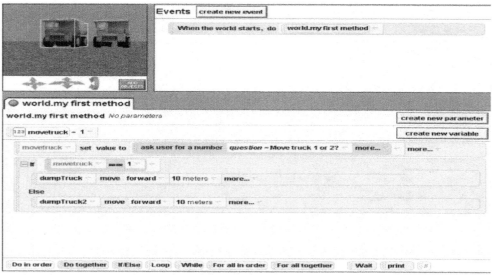

Figure 3.1.1

This example shows a few concepts in Alice programming. First, a new variable has been created called "movetruck" which is set to a value of 1. The first instruction sets the value stored in movetruck to a value entered by the user. In the World object there is a function "ask user for a number" this is dragged to replace the value of 1 and a value of "Move truck 1 or 2?" is entered as the prompt for the user to enter a number.

Then comes the IF statement. The value in movetruck is tested and if it is equal to a 1, the first dumptruck is moved forward 10 meters. Any other value will cause the second dumptruck to move forward 10 meters.

Also, decision structures can be "nested". Simply, this means that if there is an If/Else structure, there may be another If/Else structure in either or both the true statement and/or the false statements. Nesting can be as many levels of nesting as required to complete the task required by the program.

Let's use nesting to expand the previous example of the If statement. If the user enters some value other than a 1, the movetruck variable is again tested to determine if it is NOT equal to a 2. If this evaluates to a true, the camera moves back 10 meters and thinks (displays on the screen), "The directions were 1 or 2.... Pay Attention!". If the expression evaluates to false (a 2 was entered) the truck moves forward 10 meters. This limits the user to entering only a 1 or a 2 to move the appropriate truck.

Example 3.1.2 illustrates this use of nested if statements. You may nest as many if statements as necessary to achieve the desired action.

39

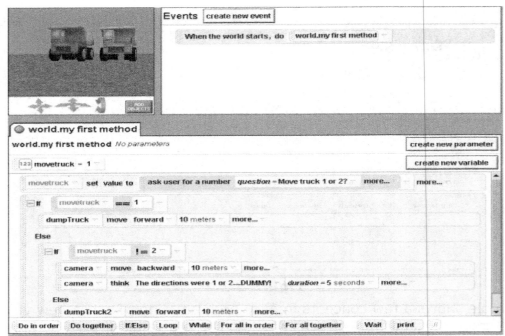

Figure 3.1.2

There are three(3) logical operators. These are used when we need to evaluate several expressions and based on the aggregate boolean evaluation the program makes a decision to do the true statements or the false statements

Logical Operators

not a   reverses the truth of expression a

both a and b   if both expressions evaluate to true it returns true any other combination of evaluations results in a return of false

        Example: 5 == 5 and 7 > 3 – both are true so the entire expression is true

                5 >= 9 and 7 > 3 – only one is true so the entire expression is false

                5 >= 9 and 3 > 7 – both are false so the entire expression is false

either a or b, or both   if the expressions both return true or if either one is true the evaluation results in a return of true. If both are false it returns false.

        Example: 5 == 5 or 7 > 3 – both are true so the entire expression is true

                5 >= 9 or 7 > 3 – only one is true so the entire expression is true

                5 >= 9 or 3 > 7 – both are false so the entire expression is false

Figure 3.1.3

Use logical operators when there are several conditions to be evaluated before the program can decide what code to execute. In the example if the user selects truck 1 and selects turn right, the truck one will move forward 10 meters, turn to the right, move forward 5 meters and dump its load. If truck 1 and turn left are selected, it will move forward 10 meters, turn left and move forward 5 meters and dump the load. If truck two is selected, the same options and actions are executed.

In Review:

3.1.1 Use _____ operators when there are several conditions to be evaluated

3.1.2 Use _____ operators to compare two values or the contents of two variables or the content of a variable and a value.

3.1.3 There are ____ logical operators.

3.1.4 There are ____ relational operators.

3.1.5 A _____ expression evaluates to either true or false.

Lesson 3.2 – Billboard

The billboard allows you to get a picture or a title into your Alice movie. Select a picture, modify or create one using a product like Microsoft Paint, Gimp, PhotoShop, or Paint.NET. I use Paint.NET to create or modify the 2D graphics in my Alice movies. It is a free download and is easy to use.

There are several common formats for pictures. GIF, PNG, JPG (or JPEG), and BMP are some of the most popular formats. Each of these has some unique characteristics that you should consider before selecting one for your Alice movie.

- GIF – Graphics Interchange Format – Used for clip art or text. Supports transparent background and is a compressed format which makes an image that less bytes for your movie. This should help keep your movie smaller in size and load faster. GIF also supports animation.
- PNG – Portable Network Graphics – Similar to GIF. Supports transparency, animation and is a compressed format. I recommend this format for use with billboards.
- JPG or (JPEG) – Joint Photographers Graphics - This is an uncompressed format that is great for high quality pictures. If you need sharp pictures with lots of colors and GIF or PNG just does not do your picture justice, choose JPG. It does not support transparency or animation.
- BMP – Bit Mapped Pictures – An uncompressed format and is usually larger than any of the other choices. Use this sparingly and preferably never.

You put the billboard on your movie set by selecting the File Menu and then clicking on the Make Billboard selection. This brings up a dialog box where you choose your picture and add it to your movie. Once on the movie set, you can position the billboard as required.

I used Paint.NET to create a movie title to add to the opening of my movie.

My First Alice Movie...

Figure 3.2.1

The next step was to place it in the movie. Using the Make Billboard selection, I added it to the movie and placed a penguin at either end of the billboard.

Figure 3.2.2

Now, add some action to the billboard using the billboard's methods and then make it disappear by setting the isShowing property to false.

Figure 3.2.3

The billboard turns to face the camera, rolls and turns. Then using the resize method it grows larger on the screen over a 5 second duration. Then, it disappears to make way for the movie.

A picture can be used for a background. I dug into my picture files and found a street scene to make a background for my next movie. A GIF or a PNG format is sufficient for a background. If you use a JPG it will take some time to save and load your project.

Figure 3.2.4

Alice and the Class Jock look as if they are standing on a street in a small town in the heart of the Berkshires of Massachusetts. This could be an opportunity to use some of those photos of scenery or perhaps use Alice to teach a history lesson at some historic site or natural wonder.

In Review:

3.2.1 The _____ allows you to get a picture or a title into your Alice movie.

3.2.2 _____ is used for clip art or text.

3.2.3 _____ is similar to GIF. Supports transparency, animation and is a compressed format.

3.2.4 You put the billboard on your movie set by selecting the _____ Menu and then clicking on the _____ _____ selection.

Lesson 3.3 – 3D Text

Put titles on movies with 3D Text. There are two ways to access 3D Text. First, the last entry in the Gallery of Objects is 3D TEXT. Clicking on this opens a dialog box. The default text in the dialog box is "The quick brown fox." and this may be changed to the appropriate text for the movie. Also, in the dialog box a font style may be selected, and buttons to display the text as bold or in italics. The second way is to select it from the menu bar. It is found under the File menu in a sub menu titled "Add 3D Text...".   Selecting this item opens the same dialog box as was opened in the first method.

3D Text has Properties, Methods, and Functions like all other objects. For example, if you want a different color text you select the color property and then select the new color. If you want the text to rotate, select a method that turns or rolls the text. Explore the methods and functions for many different things that can be done with text objects.

An example of using a picture as background with 3D text is the title for another Alice Travelogue.

Figure 3.3.1

Go back to the movie magic we played with the billboard title and do some neat effects with your own 3D titles.

In Review:

3.3.1 There are _____ ways to access 3D Text.

3.3.2 3D Text has Properties, Methods, and Functions like all other objects. (True / False)

3.3.3 3D text can be added from the "Tools" menu. (True / False)

Lesson 3.4 - Create an Alice Movie

Alice has a feature that allows the Alice movie (the .a2w file) to be turned into a movie file. Alice supports the Quicktime format .MOV. This feature allows you to share your Alice creations on YouTube or send to those who may not be able to run Alice movies from the .a2w file.

The steps are simple. Go to File and select Export Video. This will produce a dialog box like the one in Figure 3.4.1.

Figure 3.4.1

If you have not saved your changes Alice will require that you save your work before continuing.

In the dialog box in the upper left corner there is a button that is titled **Record**, click on this button. Your movie will now run. When the movie is complete you need to click on the next button, **Stop Recording**. Then over on the right top of the dialog box there is a button that is titled **Export Video**, click on this button.

Now Alice takes over and you may see a Message Box on the Screen that says **"Encoding Video"**. When the movie has been completely created you will find a .MOV file on your desktop with the same name as your Alice project.

This file can be run on any computer that can run Quicktime movies or can be uploaded to YouTube to share with all your friends on the Internet or everyone that can access YouTube.

In Review

3.4.1 Alice generates movies with the Quicktime _____ file extension.

3.4.2 Once you have clicked on the Stop Recording button, you must click on the _____ button.

Lesson 3.5 - Print Code

If a printout of all code is necessary Alice provides a way to export the code as a HTML file which can be read and printed by any browser.

Open the *File* menu item and select the *Export Code for Printing* option. This brings up a dialog box. See Figure 3.5.1

Figure 3.5.1

46

This dialog box asks you what methods you want to export, check off all for which you wish to export the code. You must type something into the box titled "Author's Name", usually your name and then click on the **"Export Code"** button. The default destination is the Desktop folder. The file will be named whatever the name was given to the Alice program with an extension of .html. The file can then be viewed in any browser and will resemble the code in Figure 3.5.2.

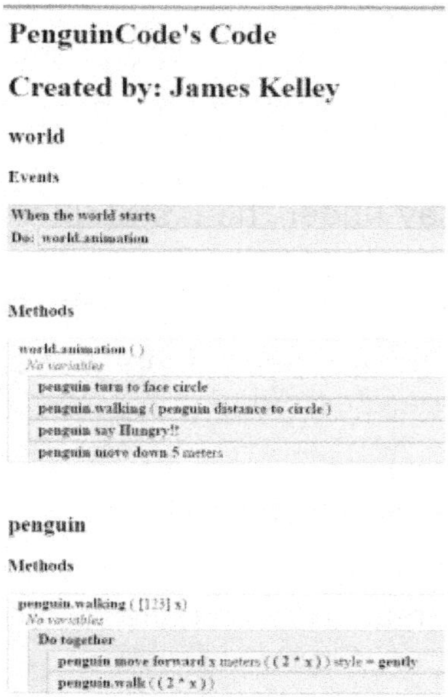

PenguinCode's Code

Created by: James Kelley

world

Events

When the world starts
Do: world.animation

Methods

world.animation ( )
  No variables
    penguin turn to face circle
    penguin walking (penguin distance to circle)
    penguin say Hungry!!
    penguin move down 5 meters

penguin

Methods

penguin.walking ([123] x)
  No variables
    Do together
      penguin move forward x meters ((2 * x)) style = gently
      penguin.walk ((2 * x))

Figure 3.5.3

In Review

3.5.1 Alice exports the print file to a file with the _____ file extension.

3.5.2 The Default directory for the print file is the _____ folder.

Lesson 3.6 - Try This

In this movie the bunny object spins based on the value of the variable named number. If the number is greater than or equal to 5, the bunny says "I don't spin more than 5 times". Run the program twice, one with answer having a value of 1 and a second run with a value of 8.

1. Create a Grass World.
2. In the upper right corner of the World Editor Area, Click on "Create New Variable"
   a. Name = answer
   b. Data Type = Number
   c. Value = 1
   d. OK
3. Add the Bunny object to the world from the Animal gallery.
4. Drag and Drop the If/Else to the first line of the World Editor and select true.
5. Drag and Drop the variable answer over "true" set to answer >= 5.
6. Select the Bunny Object
7. Drag and Drop bunny.say under the if statement but before the else. Select Other
8. MESSAGE= "I don't spin more than 5 times." Duration = 5 seconds.
9. Drag and Drop bunny.turn at speed under the else statement. Turn = left Speed = 5 revolutions per second.
10.   PLAY
11.   Change answer = 1 to answer = 8
12.   PLAY
13.   Drag and Drop the answer variable to the line just before the "If" statement. Value = 1.
14.   Select the World Object.
15.   Select Function = "ask user for a number" and drag and drop over the 1 in the variable created just above the "If" statement.
16.   PLAY Test with entering a 2 then test again entering 8
17.   Select Bunny Object and drag and drop "bunny move", forward, 10 meters.
18.   PLAY Test with entering a 2 then test again entering 8
19.   Now print all of the code generated for this project.
20.   Export this video and view it on your favorite software used to show Quicktime videos (.mov files)

Chapter 4 – Repetition

Overview:

- Explain repetition.
- Use a counter loop.
- Use a while loop.
- Describe when to use each type of loop

Lesson 4.0 – Overview of Repetition

The Last structure to be examined is the "Repetition" structure. This is the real power of a program, the ability to repeat a series of instructions. Perhaps something so simple in Alice Worlds as making an object jump up and down three times or move towards another object until you are 1 meter from the other object. These activities require using "loops" or the repetition structure.

The repetition structure tests a condition and if the condition evaluates to true, allows the program to repeat one or more times, until the condition changes and evaluates to false. However, there must be something in the loop changes the condition to avoid the "dreaded infinite loop". This is a loop that never ends because the condition to exit the loop is never met.

There are two types of loops in Alice. First, there is the LOOP structure. This structure is used when a loop is to be executed a number of times. It may be a specific number or it may use the contents of a variable. The benefit of this loop is that it uses a built in counter structure that insures the loop will be exited at some point. The second structure is the WHILE loop. This loop executes while a condition is true, false or is a compound loop selected by choosing the logic choice which then continues to asks to construct a compound loop condition. See Figure 4.0.1.

Figure 4.0.1

The Loop structure can be viewed in a simple or complex version by selecting the button at the end of the command. The complex version shows all of the components of the command and can be used to change the increment value from 1 to some other value. There is only one version of the While structure.

In Review

4.0.1 The Loop structure can be viewed in a _____ or _____ version

4.0.2 There are _____ types of loops in Alice.

4.0.3 The _____ structure tests a condition and if the condition evaluates to true, allows the program to repeat one or more times, until the condition changes and evaluates to false.

4.0.4 The _____ loop is a loop that never ends because the condition to exit the loop is never met.

4.0.5 There are also two versions of the While loop structure.   (True / False)

Lesson 4.1 Repetition (Counter Loops)

At the bottom of the Method Editor there is a tile labeled "loop". Drag this to the location in the Method Editor where the loop belong and drop it. Then, enter the number of times (iterations) the loop is to be repeated. Under that drop the appropriate instructions that are to be repeated. This builds a counter controlled loop. Generally this is written as a "For" loop in most programming languages

This type of loop may be used when an object is to do something a certain number of times. For Example: when programming an ice skating scene and the skater is to turn around three times. Either write three turn statements or simplify by writing a loop that turns the skater three times.

Perhaps this is not the best example but consider the skater is to turn the number of times contained in a variable. The number of times to turn is unknown when the program is being written. The value will be supplied when the program runs. Here is where the loop statement shines.

Consider a situation where the programmer wants the Alice character to jump up 1 meter and then back down again and do this ten times. Since the number of times is known the loop should be executed, and the LOOP structure would be selected. Could this operation be done without a loop structure? Certainly, just repeat the move up and move down instructions ten times each, but this results in twenty instructions and that is messy code. Imagine the code that would have to be written to have Alice jump up and down a thousand times. By using the LOOP structure, only three lines of code are written, no matter how many times she needs to jump. Here is the code for jumping ten times:

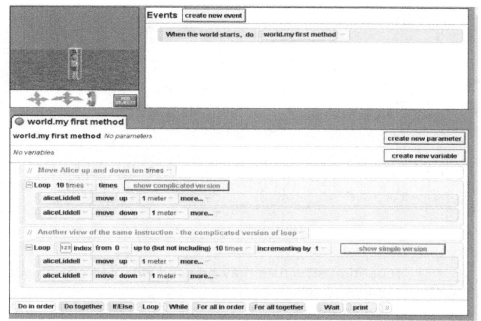

Figure 4.1.1

Note that Figure 4.0.2 shows two different views of the LOOP structure. The first is the "simple version" which shows the number of times to loop and will increment the counter by one until it reaches the stated number of times. The second is the complicated version which shows the full version. It shows three parts of the loop that can be varied that fully explain the loop structure and how it operates. First it shows that it has declared a variable named index and initialized it to zero, then it shows the condition that will cause the loop to exit (up to (but not including) 10 times. The last part is (increment by 1) where the number that we add to the variable index can be changed. So, if a positive number is entered, the program will increment through the loop and if it is a negative number the program decrements the index and count from a higher number to a lower number.

Some examples of other ways to use the loop structure:

A Loop that Decrements.

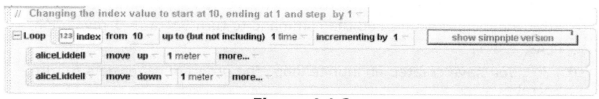

Figure 4.1.2

A Loop that Increments by 2.

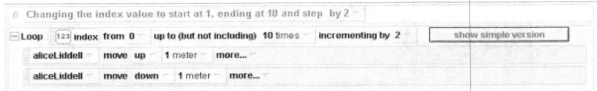

Figure 4.1.3

Note that the user could substitute a variable for any of the values and use the contents of the variable to control the starting point, the ending point or the step value.

In Review

4.1.1 The _____ repetition structure may be used when an object is to do something a certain number of times.

4.1.2 The user could substitute a _____ for any of the values and use the contents of the variable to control the starting point, the ending point or the step value.

4.1.3 Changing the incrementing by value to a _____ _____ causes the index to count from a larger number to a smaller number.

Lesson 4.2 Coding Counter Loops

1. Select a Grass World
2. Select the Socrates object from the People Gallery
3. Click on Done
4. Drag the Loop icon to the Method Editor
5. Choose "Infinity Times"
6. Now, Move Socrates forward 1 meter.
7. Move Socrates backward 1 meter.
8. After the loop structure add the command to turn Socrates 1 revolution.
9. PLAY
10. You have created an infinite loop. The program never gets to turn Socrates.
11. Stop the program.
12. Change "Infinity times" to 5.
13. PLAY

52

On the loop line click on the button that reads "Show Complicated Version". This changes the appearance of the loop line. The line now shows the structure of the "For" loop. Note the loop initializes the index variable, has a test condition to limit the process when the value of the index reaches 5 and finally an update portion telling the computer to add one to the index each time through the loop. This structure is exactly the same in JAVA, C++ and C.

Lesson 4.3 - Repetition (While Loops)

Sometimes it is necessary to perform a series of instructions based on some "boolean" condition testing "True". An Example is: "Repeat these instructions until the contents of expression A are greater than the contents of expression B". Another example would be to repeat some instructions until one object is less than one meter from a second object

The "While" loop is the tool to use for this problem. The "While" loop is a Pretest loop. This means that the condition for doing the loop instructions is evaluated before any instructions are executed. Therefore the instructions in the loop may never be executed

The tile for the while instruction is at the bottom of the Method Editor. Just as the loop instruction was implemented, drag the while tile to the appropriate place in the code. Then supply a boolean expression to be evaluated in the input box with the initial value of "true". Then follow with the instructions to be executed within the loop

Figure 4.3.1

53

The lunar lander will continue to descend a half a meter at a time to the surface (ground) while it is still above the ground the test is true. Once the test is that it is at or below the ground, the test will be false and the while loop will exit.

In Review

4.3.1 The _____ loop structure repeats instructions until the expression evaluated, evaluates to false.

4.3.2 The "While" loop is a _____-test loop.

4.3.3 The instructions in the While loop may never be executed. (True / False)

Lesson 4.4 Coding While Loops

Example using the While Loop and Random Numbers

1. Select a Grass World
2. In Animals Gallery there is a "Bugs" subdirectory. Select:
    a. georgebeetle (on the left)
    b. paulbeetle (in the center)
    c. ringobeetle (on the right)
3. Select georgebeetle and move left of paulbeetle one meter
4. Select ringobeetle and move right of paulbeetle one meter
5. Drag and Drop While Statement to next line and select true.
6. Select gerogebeetle functions and Drag and Drop "georgebeetle is at least threshold" over 'true' in while statement. At least .05 from paulbeetle, the entire paulbeetle.
7. Drag and Drop georgebeetle move left 1 meter to the while statement.
8. Select World Object, random number, and replace 1 meter in georgebeetle move left
    a. minimum = -0.5
    b. maximum = +0.5
9. After while statement Drag and drop georgebeetle say hello.
10.   PLAY (play until georgebeetle says hello)

54

Lesson 4.5 Random Numbers

The World object has a function called "random number", which returns a fractional random number between 0 and 1. The "more..." editing tag has the following arguments:

minimum   specify a minimum value for the random number to be returned.

maximum   specify a maximum value for the random number to be returned. The value returned will be a value not greater than, one less than the specified maximum number

integer only   when set to true, the function converts the value generated and returns only whole numbers.

When the problem is to have six numbers returned (simulating the roll of dice) set a minimum of one (1) and a maximum of seven (7) and integer only set to true. This will return the values 1 to 6.

Figure 4.5.1

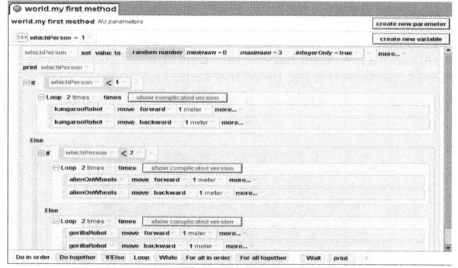

Figure 4.5.2

In Figure 4.5.1 there are three Sci-Fi characters in a line and facing the front. The program in Figure 4.5.2 is the code that randomly moves one of the three

55

characters forward and backward 2 times. A random number is generated between 0 and 3 and the result is stored in the variable "whichPerson". The print statement is used to display the random number being generated at the bottom of the movie screen. The Print command is found in a tile at the bottom of the editor. When the movie is played, it will display values or messages at the bottom of the screen. This is a debugging tool and should be removed after the results have been confirmed working. Then there is a nested if statement to decide which character should move, 0, 1 or 2.

Random numbers are especially important when writing games or when the movie requires objects moving or acting in a random manner.

In Review

4.5.1 Random Number is a function of the _____ _____.

4.5.2 The Print command displays values on the default printer. (True / False)

4.5.3 The maximum number limits the highest number returned to one less than the maximum number specified. (True / False)

4.5.4 The _____ _____ function returns a fractional number between 0 and 1.

Lesson 4.6 – Lists

Alice has the ability to create a variable as a list. List variables have the ability to store multiple items of the same data type. The list can then be used to step through the items one at a time, having that item perform some task. One rule is that your list can contain any objects. They do not need to be all the same. Another is that all items in the list be of the same data type.

Our example for this lesson is to build a water world for three boats.

Figure 4.6.1

Line up three sailboats facing the camera. The first boat is on the left, the second in the middle and the third on the right. The objective of the movie is to have each sailboat turn right one quarter turn and sail off the screen. Instead of six instructions to do this we will set up a list of boats and each will sail off in turn.

To set up the list variable we need to create a new variable. Because the variable may be used throughout the movie we need to set up a variable under the world object. Select the world object in the object tree and then go to the properties. Click on "create a new variable" and get the dialog box in Figure 4.6.2. Name the variable, select the object radio button, click on the check box to the left of "make a" and make sure the list box contains "List". Then click on the "new item" button three times. Next to item0's None, click on the drop down arrow and select the first sailboat. Then repeat for the second and third sailboats. When complete, your dialog box should look like Figure 4.6.2. If all is ok, click on OK.

Figure 4.6.2

Now we can use the variable in our code. The "For all in order" structure executes the commands for all items in the list in sequence. All the commands for the first item, then all the commands for the next item and continues until the list is finished. Grab the tile "For all in order" from the bottom of the event panel. Select the boat list by selecting the world.boatList. Now, we have a loop structure to carry out our commands to be done by each member of the list.

Note there is no object in the object tree, so where do we get the method to move our sailboats? Easy, look in the code line that begins with "For all...". There is an object variable named "item_from_boatList". Drag this down one line to the "Do Nothing.." area. Select turn, right and 0.25 revolutions. Repeat this process using the move method, forward and 100 meters.

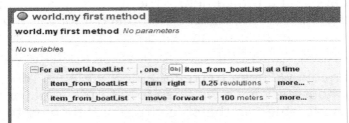

Figure 4.6.3

Play the movie and watch your boats turn to their right and sail off the screen.

Figure 4.6.4

If the boats don't sail in the correct order you can fix the order in the list variable.

The other command for list processing is the "For All Together..." command. This is used when all members of the list should act at the same time. Our example for this is a simple "Chicken Dance."

Figure 4.6.5

We have three chickens in a row. The code begins with selecting the tile "For All Together..." from the tiles across the bottom. Using the same procedure as was used for "For all in order..." build the movements for the dance.

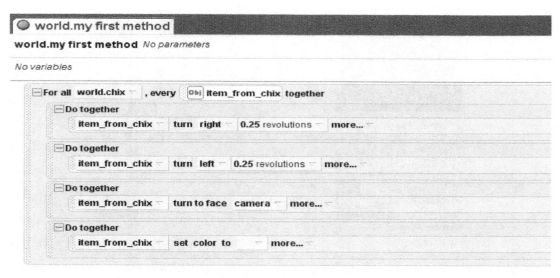

Figure 4.6.6

Just some simple movements to illustrate how the dance may begin. Turning yellow at the end was just added to illustrate property changes for all items in the list.

In Review

4.6.1 _____ variables have the ability to store multiple items.

4.6.2 The _____ structure executes the commands for all items in the list in sequence.

4.6.3 The _____ structure is used when all members of the list should act at the same time.

Lesson 4.7 – Arrays

An array is like a list. It is used to hold a group of like items. It has a fixed size and once it has been filled you can't add any more new items. An array is composed of a group of elements. An element is a storage place for each item in the array.

When you insert an item into an array, it does not shift in position like in a list. In an array you insert the value into a specific element where it remains until changed, or deleted.

The first element in an array is item0, the second, item1, the third item2 and so on.

To create an array, click on "create new variable" button in the object or method where you want to create the array. Name the variable, select the type of item you want to store in the array. Then click the "make a" option and select Array in the drop down list. The dialog box will expand to allow you to Add New Items. Add as many items as you need to put in the array. Click on OK to create the array.

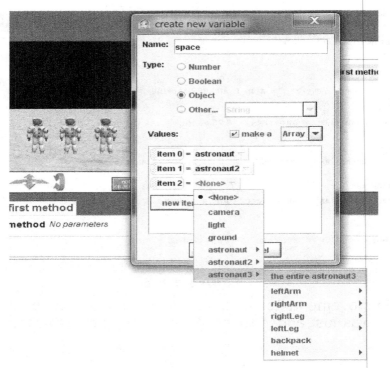

Figure 4.7.1

The array is listed in the object or method where it was created. The asterisk (*) next to the name indicates it is an array. (See Figure 4.7.2) Once completed this array can be used in your program. The example in Figure 4.7.3 shows using the array in a Loop.

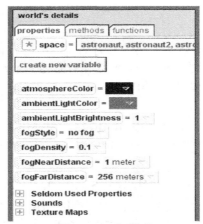

Figure 4.7.2

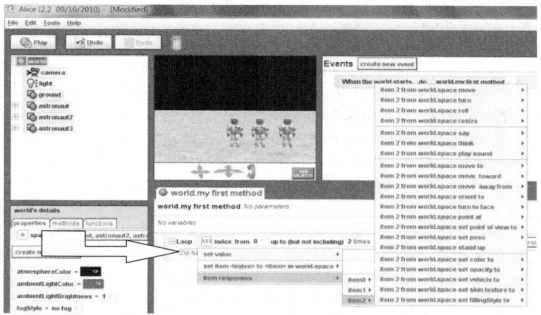

Figure 4.7.3

When you drag the space variable to the "Do Nothing" line you are presented with a series of options. Select the option for the action you wish to take. There are lots of options, it is worthwhile to experiment with some of them.

In Review

4.7.1 An _____ is like a list. It is used to hold a group of like items.

4.7.2 An _____ is a storage place for each item in the array.

4.7.3 The array is listed in the object or method where it was created. The _____ next to the name indicates it is an array.

4.7.4 The first element in an array is item1,   (True / False)

4.7.5 An _____ has a fixed size and once it has been filled you can't add any more new items.

Lesson 4.8 – Try This

1. Open Alice and create a Water World.

2. Go to the Gallery and Select Environment and the select the Island.

3. Go to the People Gallery and select the ScubaDiver.. Position the ScubaDiver on the Island.

4. Go to the Animals Gallery and select the Shark. Position the Shark in front of the island, partially submerged in the water.

5. In the methods editor create the following code
    1. Loop 5 times
    2. shark turns right 1 revolution, duration 6 seconds
    3. Nest a loop that loops 2 times
        1. ScubaDiver says "Shark Attack!"
        2. camera move back 5 meters
        3. camera move forward 5 meters
6. Play the Movie.

Chapter 5 – Methods

Objectives

- Create a custom class-level method
- Use a custom method
- Pass an argument to a method
- Use the camera for effects

Lesson 5.0 - Overview of Methods

While the various classes include many methods (things they can do), there are other things that could be included as methods that would streamline our programming. So, if a class does not have a method to perform a certain task, and the task will be done repeatedly in the program and perhaps in other programs, the programmer needs to create a new method. Alice allows the programmer to create custom methods for a class.

This lesson is to learn how to create custom class-level methods in Alice.

The penguin object has a walk method. This method, when invoked, simulates the penguin walking across the stage. Other objects do not have a similar method. So, when Alice Liddel moves, her legs remain stationary and she looks like she is floating forward. This detracts from the realism of the movie.

This is an opportunity to create a method for an object to "teach" an object to walk. This is where code becomes complicated.

In Lesson 5.2 code is generated to make the Toy Soldier to "March" across the screen. This involves moving the arms and the legs appropriately to make them look like his arms and legs are moving in a realistic manner.   To keep it simple, and reduce the number of instructions, the arms and legs move as one and the bends at the knee and elbow have not been considered. However, with a little practice and patience the movement can be made even more realistic.

In Review

5.0.1 Alice allows the programmer to create custom _____ for a class.

5.0.2 The _____ object is an example of a object with a walk method.

Lesson 5.1 - Creating Custom Class-Level Methods

Methods that are part of a class are referred to as class-level methods. If there is some action that requires writing lots of code to do repeatedly, it would be beneficial to create a new class to do that action and then call that method each time the object needs to perform those steps. An example of this might be to write classes to move the soldier's legs to make him march across the screen.

There are five (5) steps to write a custom class-level method in Alice:

1. Create an instance of the class.
2. Select the instance.
3. In the Details Panel, under the methods tab, click the create new method button.
4. In the resulting dialog box, enter a unique and descriptive name for the method you wish to create, click the OK button and the new name will appear above the button in the Details Panel.
5. Create the instructions for the method in the new Method Editor.

Once created, the new method can be used just like any other methods already provided. Drag it to the methods editor and drop in the desired position.

In Review

5.1.1 Methods that are part of a class are referred to as
_____.

5.1.2 It would be beneficial to create a new _____ to do that action and then call that _____ each time the object needs to perform those steps.

5.1.3 Once created, the new method can be used just like any other methods already provided. (True / False)

Lesson 5.2   Create a Custom Class-Level Method

Create a "Sand World" and place the ToySoldier Class from the People Gallery on the sand. Now, click on Done and begin writing a method that will make the soldier March across the sand. If the move forward method was used alone, the soldier would kind of float across the sand and would not look like he is marching. This method will add some reality to this simple little movie.

Now, select the toySoldier object and click on the methods tab in the Details Panel. Click on the button to create a new method, name the new method "march". Look in the object tree at the ToySoldier object and note the plus sign (+) to the left of the name of the class. This indicates that this class is made up of several other classes. If the plus sign is selected, these sub classes will be displayed. Each of these sub classes also have properties, methods and functions attached to them. It is necessary to use several of the sub classes of the toySoldier, leftLeg, rightLeg, leftArm and rightArm.

The contents of the method are four "Do Together" sequences. In each sequence the soldier will move forward .25 meters, move his leftLeg, rightLeg, leftArm and rightArm in an appropriate distance. The legs and arms will "turn" .1 (note it is point 1) revolutions in each instruction over a duration of .5 (note it is point 5) seconds. Let's examine the code that makes this all happen.

```
do together

toySoldier.move forward .25 meters style=abruptly duration = .5
seconds more...

toySoldier.leftLeg.turn forward .1 revolutions style=abruptly duration
= .5 seconds more...

toySoldier.rightLeg.turn backward .1 revolutions style=abruptly
duration = .5 seconds more...

toySoldier.leftArm.turn forward .1 revolutions style=abruptly duration
= .5 seconds more...

toySoldier.rightArm.turn backward .1 revolutions style=abruptly
duration = .5 seconds more...

do together

toySoldier.move forward .25 meters style=abruptly duration = .5
seconds more...

toySoldier.leftLeg.turn backward .1 revolutions style=abruptly
duration = .5 seconds more...

toySoldier.rightLeg.turn forward .1 revolutions style=abruptly
duration = .5 seconds more...

toySoldier.leftArm.turn backward .1 revolutions style=abruptly
duration = .5 seconds more...

toySoldier.rightArm.turn forward .1 revolutions style=abruptly
duration = .5 seconds more...

do together

toySoldier.move forward .25 meters style=abruptly duration = .5
seconds more...

toySoldier.leftLeg.turn backward .1 revolutions style=abruptly
duration = .5 seconds more...

toySoldier.rightLeg.turn forward .1 revolutions style=abruptly
duration = .5 seconds more...

toySoldier.leftArm.turn backward .1 revolutions style=abruptly
duration = .5 seconds more...

toySoldier.rightArm.turn forward .1 revolutions style=abruptly
duration = .5 seconds more...

do together

toySoldier.move forward .25 meters style=abruptly duration = .5
seconds more...

toySoldier.leftLeg.turn forward .1 revolutions style=abruptly duration
= .5 seconds more...

toySoldier.rightLeg.turn backward .1 revolutions style=abruptly
duration = .5 seconds more...

toySoldier.leftArm.turn forward .1 revolutions style=abruptly duration
= .5 seconds more...
```

```
toySoldier.rightArm.turn backward .1 revolutions style=abruptly
duration = .5 seconds more...
```

Now, we have a method named "march" and we can use this method just as we would use any other method for that class. This may look like a lot of code and it is, that is why we code these routines once and reuse whenever possible.

Lesson 5.3 Using the Method

With the new method ready to go, return to the "world.my first method" and use the method just like it was one of the methods that were programmed into the toySoldier class.

To keep things simple, will loop through executing the method ten times. This simply requires dragging the "Loop" structure from the bottom of the methods editor and selecting 10 times. Then simply drag and drop the "march" function created beneath the Loop structure and the toy soldier is ready to march across the screen. Hit the PLAY button and if it is all correct, your soldier marches across the screen.

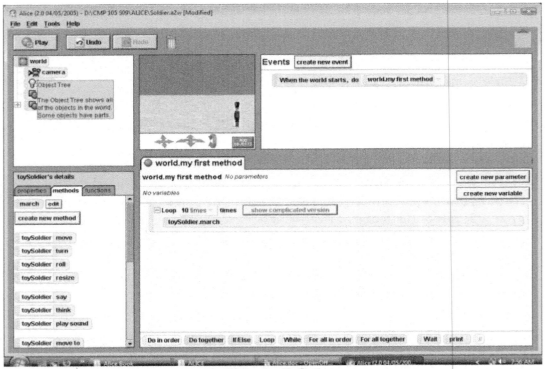

Figure 5.3.1

Lesson 5.4 – Passing Arguments to Methods

Sometimes it is necessary for the calling program to pass information (or values) to the called method. This is called passing an argument to a method.

If a method is to accept an argument when it is called, it is necessary to create a parameter in the method. A parameter is simply a variable that can hold the value of the argument when it is passed.

To create a parameter in a method, there is a "Create New Parameter" button in the method editor for creating a parameter variable to hold the argument passed from the calling method. Clicking on this button opens a dialog box identical to the one opened for a new variable. Enter a name, select a type and create a parameter variable.

Once this has been done, an argument will be required each time the method is called.

Figure 5.4.1

Figure 5.4.1 shows the SoldierSpin method that asks for a parameter named spinTimes.

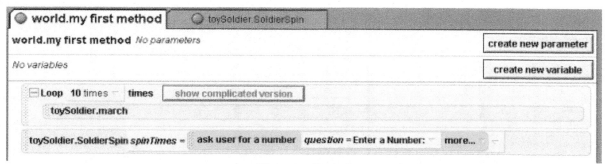

Figure 5.4.2

Figure 5.4.2 shows the SoldierSpin method used in the program. The ToySoldier will march forward and when he stops, the user will be requested to enter a number and the ToySoldier will turn that many times.

In Review

5.4.1 If a method is to accept an argument when it is called, it is necessary to create a _____ in the method.

5.4.2 Sometimes it is necessary for the calling program to pass information (or values) to the called method. This is called passing an _____ to a method.

Lesson 5.5 Using the Camera

The World View is the camera's viewfinder. The viewpoint of the camera is its current position and the direction in which it is pointed. There are several ways to control the camera. First in design mode there are the three camera controls (sets of arrows) at the bottom of the screen.

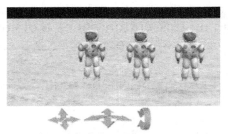

Figure 5.5.1

Left to right the controls are:

- up, down, left, right
- forward, backward, rotate left, rotate right
- tilts the camera up or down

The second method is moving the camera in the program. The camera is listed in the object tree and has properties, methods and functions. Let's look at the methods and functions available.

Figure 5.5.2

68

Once again there are too many options to explain. You need to experiment with these options in your movies to take advantage of the effects they can add to your movie. Create a scene and then add code to control the camera and experiment with the effects you can create using the camera.

In Review

5.5.1 The _____ _____ is the camera's viewfinder.

5.5.2 The camera is listed in the object tree and has _____, _____, and _____.

Lesson 5.6 Try This

This exercise causes a character to jump up and down a specified number of times.

1. Select the Dir World
2. Place the Class Ant on the world.
3. Select the Class Ant instance.
4. Click on Create New Method
5. Create New Parameter - jtime - type number
6. Loop jtime times
7. ant move up 1 meter
8. ant move down 1 meter
9. Return to world.my first method
10. Drag and Drop jump method to the method editor.
11. Select 2
12. PLAY

Add another jump method to the program with a different value. PLAY again.

Chapter 6 – Functions

Objectives

- Differentiate a function from a method
- Create a movie that uses functions
- Use functions in calculations.

Lesson 6.0 – Overview of Functions

The Functions Tab defines functions as "Functions are the things that an object can answer about themselves or the world."

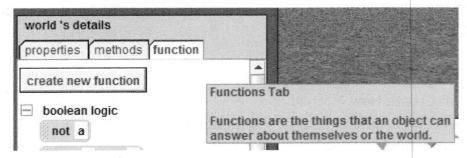

Figure 6.0.1 – The Functions Tab

Functions differ from Methods in that methods do some task or operation while a function returns some information about the world or its objects. These functions ask a question and return a value which can be a number, and object, a Boolean (true or false), or some other object type.

Functions can optionally accept values in the form of arguments (or parameters). Then return some value as output using the required ***return*** statement. There are built-in functions for every object as well as the capability to create new functions.

Some functions for example, calculate the distance between one object and another object. Another example is a function returns a random number. A third example is a function that calculates a value and returns it to the calling program.

In Review

6.0.1 A _____ returns some information about the world or its objects.

6.0.2 A _____ does some task or operation.

6.0.3 A value is returned to the calling statement using the _____ statement.

Lesson 6.1 – Built-In Functions – World

If we look at the "World" object we see a general set of functions. These functions differ from functions we see for other objects. These functions have to do with the categories: boolean logic, math, random numbers, strings, ask user, mouse, time, advanced math, and other. World functions are generally used for values that may pertain to several different objects, user interface, and math functions. The Figure 6.1.1 shows a partial list of the world functions.

Figure 6.1.1 – World Functions

As you can see there are functions that apply to many different situations. Generating a random number, asking the user for a number or a string, converting a number to a string are just a few examples of the world's functions. These functions apply to many different situations and this is the only place you will find these functions.

A popular use of a world function is the generation of a random number. There are many instances where it is necessary to have a random number generated for an object. The random number function exists ONLY in the World's functions list.

The code example has the car move forward a random distance, in meters, each time the command is executed. The parameters issued to the random function is a minimum number of 5, a maximum number of 50, and return only an integer value.

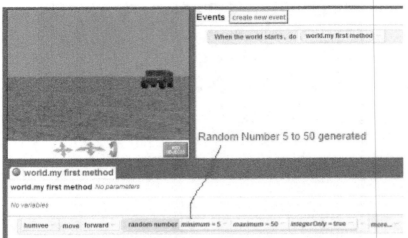

Figure 6.1.2 – Code for a World Function

As you learn more about Alice, you will find more use for these world level functions.

In review

6.1.1 The random-number function is only in the _____ function list.

6.1.2 World functions are used for _____ interface.

Lesson 6.2 – Built-In Functions in Other Objects.

Most of the other objects functions have the same, or similar, function. The categories of these functions are: proximity, size, spatial relations, point of view, and other. They answer questions like "how far is this object from another object?", or "is this object to the left or right of another object?", and other similar questions about the object's relationship to the environment.

In the code example we move the sheriff to within 1 meter of the cowboy. Remember, the distance is measured from the center point of the sheriff to the center point of the cowboy.

Figure 6.2.1 – Built-In Code for Objects

The function "sheriff distance to cowboy" returns the distance between the center point of the sheriff and the center point of the cowboy. So at the end of the function 1 meter is subtracted from the value returned. You could also subtract the "width of the cowboy", which may be a more accurate value for placement.

There are many functions for each object the following is a partial, typical list containing functions that pertain to most objects.

Figure 6.2.2 – Alice Object Functions

These functions are the same in most of the objects. Remember, a function always returns a value.

In review

6.2.1 Functions measure distance from _____ to _____.

6.2.2 _____ answer questions about the object's relationship to the environment.

Lesson 6.3 – Create a New Function

As with methods, you can create a new function for an object. There may be an instance where there is an object that does not have a function that you use frequently with that object. This is the time to create a new function.

Our example will be a function to calculate how many gumdrops are in a container given the weight in ounces of the container.

The stage is a grass world with the Class Pj from the People Gallery, the GumDrop from the Kitchen Gallery (food folder), and the bag is from the Shapes Gallery the Box Class with the property value changed to brown.

The pseudocode for this game is as follows:

1. Pj announces the game

2. Ask the user for a weight in ounces.

3. Pass weight to world function calcGumDrops

4. Display answer returned from the function

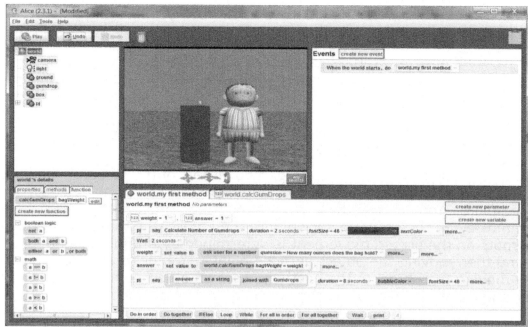

Figure 6.3.1 – Code for Movie

The world function to calculate the number of gumdrops simply divides the weight in ounces by the weight of a gumdrop which we know is .05 ounces. The function should look something like this:

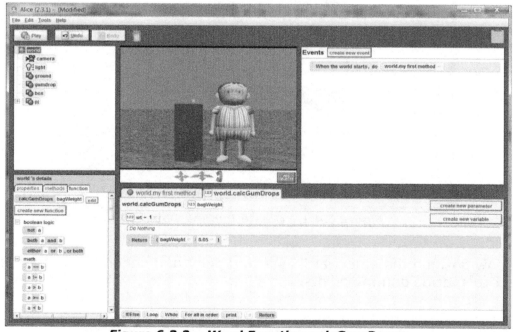

Figure 6.3.2 – Word Function calcGumDrops

This is a very simple function but it illustrates the use of a function to do a calculation. The function returns the contents of the parameter passed divided by the numeric literal 0.05 which is the weight of one gumdrop.

75

In Review

6.3.1 A function always returns a _____.

6.3.2 A _____ is a value passed to the function.

Lesson 6.4 – Dummy Objects.

Often you want to move an object to a particular part of the screen. Alice has the ability to set points on the screen called "dummy objects" and objects can "move to" these points. You can use these points to position objects at various times during a movie. In the scenario shown here the object (the mummy) moves to several spots on the screen movement is determined by dropping points on the screen and then moving the object to these points. You generate these dummy spots by moving the object to the spot you want an object to move to and then dropping the dummy object using the button on the Add Objects screen.

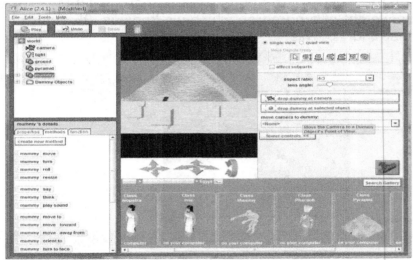

Figure 6.4.1 – Create Dummy Objects

You can now position the object at its starting point and generate the code to move the object to specific dummy points.

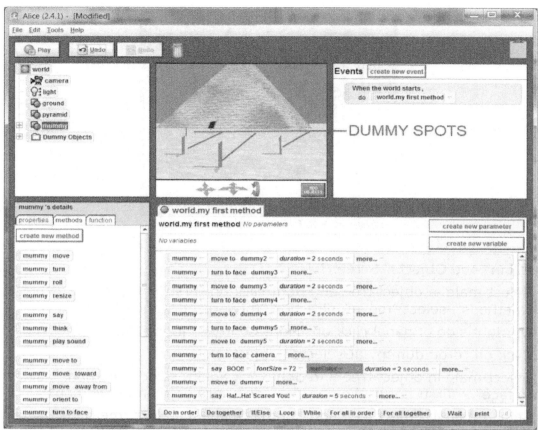

Figure 6.4.2 – Location of Dummy Spots and Code

Use the "move to" command and select the appropriate dummy spot as the destination. I did not rename the dummy spots but if there are a number of spots it may be a good idea. You may also use these dummy spots to relocate the camera.

In Review

6.4.1 _____ _____ are points on the screen used to control the movement of objects.

6.4.2 Use the _____ ____ command to move the object to a dummy object.

Lesson 6.5 – Try This

Open a new "Sand" World and go to "Add Objects" screen, select the Ancients Collection. Add Class Shelter, Class Apple Tree, Add FirstCenturyMale2, and FirstCenturyWoman1 as shown in Figure 6.5.1.

77

Figure 6.5.1 – Starting positions

While still in "Add Objects" Screen:

1. Select male in object tree and right click on "firstCenturyMale2", select "methods", select "move", direction "forward", distance "10 meters".

2. On right side of panel click on "More Controls" if not already selected.

3. Click on "drop dummy at selected object" button.

4. Select male in object tree and right click again, select "methods", select "turn to face" - "firstCenturyWoman1" - "the entire firstcenturywoman1".

5. Select male in object tree and right click again, select "methods", select "move to" - "firstcenturywoman1" – the "entire firstcenturywoman1".

6. Now you will see the two objects overlap. Move the firstcenturymale2 a short distance away from the woman.

7. Click on "drop dummy at selected object" button.

8. Select woman in object tree and right click on "firstCenturyWoman1", select "methods", select "turn to face" - "firstCenturyMale2" - "the entire firstcenturymale2.

9. Move the male object back to his original position.

Almost ready to code but first go to the object tree and select the male object, select "methods", select "turn to face", select "Dummy objects", select "dummy". Then click on the GREEN "DONE" button and put the following code in the world.myfirstmethod.

1. Have the male "move to" the Dummy object named "dummy".

2. Have the male "turn to face" the "firstCenturyWoman1", the "entire firstcenturyWoman1.

3. Have the male "move to" the Dummy object named "dummy2".

4. Have the male object say "Hello!"
5. Now PLAY.

Your screen should look like the screen shown in Figure 6.5.2

Figure 6.5.2 – Final Screen

Chapter 7 – Events

Objectives

- Describe various events
- Create a movie that uses several events
- Explain why events are important in Alice

Lesson 7.0 – Overview of Events

An event is an action that takes place while the Alice world is playing. Alice worlds are capable of recognizing certain events and responding to them. This is also important to understand for other languages that implement "Event Driven" programming, like Visual Basic.NET and other "Visual" languages

The "Event Editor" area is in the top right portion of the screen. When an Alice world is first opened, one event will be listed in this area. When the movie starts, do "world.my first method " is the method invoked by default.

Events Alice can Detect

- When the world starts
- When a key is typed
- When the mouse is clicked on something
- While something is true
- When a variable changes
- Let the mouse move <object>
- Let the arrow keys move <subject>
- Let the mouse move the camera
- Let the mouse orient the camera

The "Create New Event" button allows the user to choose these events.

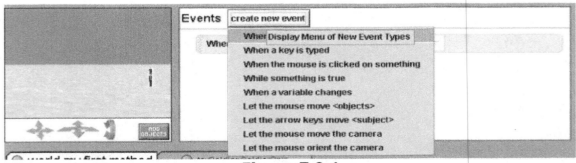

Figure 7.0.1

Using these events allows the programmer to build user interaction into the movie. An object can move as directed by the keyboard or objects can be positioned with the mouse. In addition, certain changes in the program like a variable change or something becomes true or false can be used to control what is happening on the stage.

In Review

7.0.1 Alice worlds are capable of recognizing certain _____ and responding to them.

7.0.2 When the movie starts, do "_____ " is the method invoked by default.

7.0.3 Using events allows the programmer to build user _____ into the movie.

7.0.4 The "_____" button allows the user to choose these events.

Lesson 7.1 - Using Events

Knowing when to use an event is key to Alice programming. Events must be carefully planned so the event produces the correct responses when the program is run.

The event "When the world starts" is the event that is used by default. Every program run to date is part of this event. This lesson will expand that to encompass other events.

There are keyboard events, mouse events and events that occur during program execution:

- Events that occur during program execution.
    - When the world starts
    - While something is true
    - When a variable changes
- Keyboard Events
    - When a key is typed
    - Let the arrow keys move <subject>
- Mouse Click Events
    - Let the mouse move <object>
    - Let the mouse move the camera
    - Let the mouse orient the camera

The "Create New Event" button allows you to choose these events.

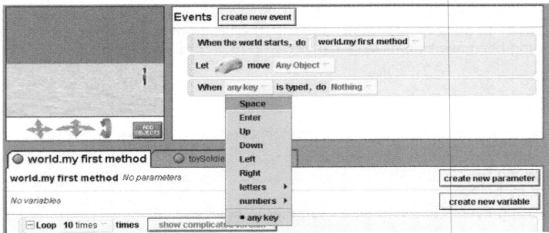

Figure 7.1.1

In Review

7.1.1 There are three categories of events:

_____

_____

_____

7.1.2 The "_____" button allows you to choose these events.

7.1.3 The event "_____" is the event that is used by default.

Lesson 7.2 Program Generated Events

- When the world starts
- While something is true
- When a variable changes

When the world starts - is the event that is generated when Alice first opens a new world. This event is triggered when the play button is pressed.   This is the default event for every program.

While something is true - While some condition is true, perform the action(s) in the called method. This will allow an event to continue as long as a condition is true which gives the same effect as a loop.

When a variable changes - This event allows for calling a method every time the contents of a variable changes. Monitors a variable and when it changes the method for this event is triggered.

In Review

7.2.1 This event is called every time the contents of a variable changes

7.2.2 The _____ event is triggered when the play button is pressed.

7.2.3 In this event the action is performed as long as the condition evaluates to true.

Lesson 7.3 - Keyboard Events

- When a key is typed
- Let the arrow keys move <subject>

When a key is typed - This allows for a method to be called in response to the user pressing one of the keys on the keyboard.

This event is valuable to allow the user to initiate some action by pressing a key. Perhaps a response to a on screen prompt or to cause the start of some portion of the movie. The old "press any key to continue" routine.

Let the arrow keys move <subject> - This event should be used with caution. An object moves under control of the arrow keys. An object may be lost while moving it with the arrow keys and miss the animations that are currently running.

Many programs allow the users to control object movement from the arrow keys. This has been the prime keyboard control since the early DOS "Alien Attack" games. The caution to use these keys carefully is that this is a 3D world. There are many ways an object can be lost in the 3D environment. The down arrow could allow the object to move below the ground and when an object disappears, the user, effectively, loses control. So, the caution is that if these arrows are used, it is a good idea to provide a way for the user to reset or find lost objects.

In Review

7.3.1 The _____ event allows for a method to be called in response to the user pressing one of the keys on the keyboard.

7.3.2 The _____ event should be used with caution.

Lesson 7.4 - Mouse Events

- Let the mouse move <object>
- Let the mouse move the camera
- Let the mouse orient the camera

Let the mouse move <objects> - This event automatically calls an internal Alice method that moves the object in a drag-and-drop manner.

This event allows the user to move objects around the stage. Just click on the object and drag it to a new location.

Let the mouse move the camera - This allows the mouse to "steer" the camera. It will be possible to move the camera off the animations presented by the world. Choosing this option allows the user to control the camera with the mouse. Allows the user to move the camera to find objects or move to another area of the stage.

Let the mouse orient the camera - This should be used with caution. It is easy to move the camera out of range of the animation and loose the effects of the rest of the movie. This allows the user to change the direction in which the camera is pointed by clicking and dragging the mouse.

In Review

7.4.1 The _____ event automatically calls an internal Alice method that moves the object in a drag-and-drop manner.

7.4.2 The _____ event allows the mouse to "steer" the camera.

Lesson 7.5 – Audio

The age of silent movies has long passed. To make movies really interesting we need to add sound. Alice makes provisions for sound but very few objects have any sounds included. You can identify objects with sound when you place them on the screen by looking at the description in dialog box that pops up when you select the object.

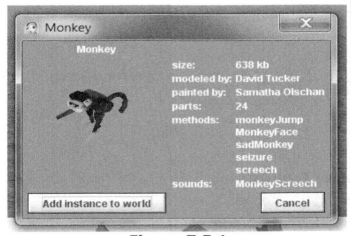

Figure 7.5.1

Note right above the Cancel button is an entry that is titled sounds and includes "MonkeyScreech". This is the only sound available as part of this object.

The good news is that you can add your own sounds with two other choices when you place the object in your movie. In the properties tab there are choices to

84

import sound or record sound for many Alice objects, including those that already have sounds.

You can import a .wav or .mp3 into your movie. When you select import you will get a dialog box that will allow you to browse to your sound and import it. This can be done in the properties tab or when you drag the "play sound" command to the editor.

Recording a sound can be done if your computer has a microphone. Select record sound from the properties tab or when you drag the play sound to the editor. A dialog box appears that allows you to record your sound. A counter will remind you how long the sound clip will play.

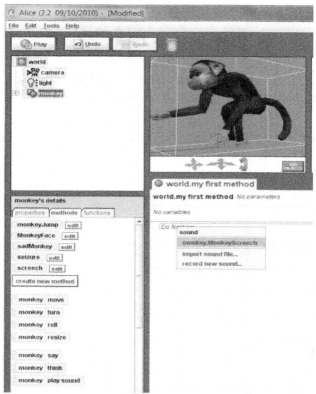

Figure 7.5. 2

Figure 7.5.3

As you see in Figure 7.5.2, we have dragged "monkey play sound" to the event editor and it asks, do we want to play the screech, import a sound or record a sound.

When the screech sound was selected the instruction appears as shown in Figure 7.5.3.

In Review

7.5.1 To make movies really interesting we need to add _____.

7.5.2 You can identify objects with sound
_____.

7.5.3   You can add your own sounds in _____ different ways.

7.5.4 You can import a _____ or _____ into your movie.

Lesson 7.6 – Wait

The Wait instruction is designed to make the program do nothing for a specified amount of time. The tile is located at the bottom of the event editor. It takes one argument, the number of seconds to wait. The program will pause and do nothing for that number of seconds.

In Review

7.6.1 The Wait instruction takes _____ argument(s).

Lesson 6.7 - Try This

This exercise creates a space scene that uses the mouse to move objects, arrow keys to move the lunarLander and when the user hits the "Q" key the lunarLander blasts off.

1. Select the Space World
2. Place the lunarLander object in the world
3. Place the astronaut object in the world
4. world.my first world method
   a. world set fogFarDistance to 75 meters
5. In Event Window Click on: Create New Event
   a. Let the mouse move <objects>
6. In Event Window Click on: Create New Event
   a. let Arrow keys move <subject>
   b. Select lunarLander
7. In the World Methods Tab: Create New Method
   a. Name the method blastoff
   b. In the method Loop 15 times
   c. In the method under Loop: lunarLander move up 0.5 meters
   d. duration = 0.25 seconds
8. In Event Window Click on: Create New Event
   a. When a key is typed
   b. Change "anykey" to "Q"
   c. Change "nothing" to blastoff

PLAY and experiment with moving objects with the mouse, use the arrow keys to move the lunarLander. Then use the "Q" key to blast off the lunarLander.

Chapter 8 – Classes

Objectives

- Explain the concept of objects and inheritance.
- Create a new method that requires a parameter.
- Create a new method for a class.
- Create a new class from an existing class.

Lesson 8.0 - Overview of Classes

A class defines a particular kind of object. The Alice programming language has classes that are predefined. These are the 3D classes found in the gallery. There are classes stored in groups like Animals, People, Environment, Buildings, etc

A class is like a recipe. It is the procedure that is used to create a new instance of that class. It contains all of the properties, methods and functions that have been assigned to that class. When one of these classes are placed on the Alice world the program is simply building that object according to the rules of that class. As many of the class can be built as needed. Just like the recipe example, one can make as many pies out of a pie recipe as they care to make.

A class may be made up of several other classes. When we look in the Object Tree, we see a plus sign (+) next to most of the objects. Clicking on that plus sign will expose all of those classes that make up the new class of object. Just like a pie consists of a recipe for crust and another for the filling and it takes both objects to create the new object, most of the Alice objects are made up of several classes.

In Review

8.0.1 A _____ is like a recipe.

8.0.2 A class may be made up of several other _____.

8.0.3 Clicking on that _____ _____ next to the object name in the object tree will expose all of those classes that make up the new class of object.

8.0.4 A _____ is a procedure that is used to create a new instance of that class.

Lesson 8.1 - Objects

When adding an instance of a class to the Alice world it already knows how to do some things like move, turn, say, roll, etc.. A previous lesson covered how to write new methods for a class to make it do more that the original methods it came with. Like the soldier in Lesson 4, we gave that object a march method that simulated the toy soldier marching across the screen. If additional toy soldiers were created on the screen, he would be the only one with the ability to march unless all were given the same march method. Since re-usability is the key in object oriented programming, Alice has a fix for this. Just like when new instances are created of each class, each inherits all of the properties, methods and functions of the original class. If a method is created for a new instance of the class, that instance may be saved as a new class and the new class will "inherit" all of the parameters, methods and functions of the original class as well as the new methods, parameters and functions just created for the new class.

The skater has been used in some of the previous exercises and when she skates, she kind of moves across the ice without simulating all of the leg and arm movements generally associated with a skater skating. Most objects have a move method that simply moves the object. The penguin is an exception since he has a walk method that moves his legs and arms as he moves. A prior lesson gave the toy soldier a march method. If there is a car or a truck it looks better moving than an animated object like people and animals but still, the wheels should turn as the vehicle moves. The biplane moves forward but would be more realistic if the propeller moved also.

The next lesson will teach an object to do a new complex action, save it as a new object so it can pass this complex action on to subsequent instances of this new class.

In Review

8.1.1   If a method is created for a new instance of the class, that instance may be saved as a _____ _____.

8.1.2 the new class will "_____" all of the parameters, methods and functions of the original class as well as the new methods, parameters and functions just created for the new class.

8.1.3 Just like when new instances are created of each class, each inherits all of the _____, _____, and _____ of the original class.

Lesson 8.2 - Inheritance

When we look at all the components of the Ice Skater found in the People Gallery, we find it is composed of other objects. The best way to view this is to put the skater object in a world and then look at the object tree.

Figure 8.2.1

There are over 30 objects that make up the IceSkater. The IceSkater object *inherits* all of the capabilities (functions, methods, properties) of all the other objects. Everything the foot object can do, it can do at the end of the right leg or the left leg. All are inherited by the IceSkater object.

Look at all of the objects that compose the upperBody object in the IceSkater. All of the things that can be done by the head object are inherited from all of the objects that compose the head object. By manipulating the properties, methods and functions lifelike actions can be attributed to the IceSkater object.

Examine other objects in the gallery and you will find that all of these objects are made up of other object. Every property, method, and function of each of the objects that make up the main object are inherited by the object you place on your world.

So, when you add a function or method to an object and compose a new class of that object, all future instances of that object inherits the new function or method.

In Review

8.2.1 When we look at all the components of an object, we find it is composed of
_____ _____.

8.2.2 By manipulating the _____, _____, and _____ other actions can be attributed to the various objects.

8.2.3 When you add a function or method to an object and compose a new class of that object, all future instances of that object inherits the new function or method. (True / False)

Lesson 8.3 – Class-Level Methods

Using the ice skater generate a new method that will simulate the more complex movements that will add realism to the action of skating across the pond. This requires more complex animations that make those Pixar movies look so real. The steps of the skating action are put together in a sequence of motions that that must be programmed into a Class-Level Method. Below are the steps to include in this new method.

- Skate
    - Do together
    - Move skater forward 2 meters
        - Do in order
            - *slide on left leg (function candidate)*
                - Do in order
                    - Lift right leg and turn upper body forward
                    - Lower right leg and turn upper body backward

90

- *slide on right leg (function candidate)*
  - Do in order
    - Lift left leg and turn upper body forward
    - Lower left leg and turn upper body backward

Now it is time to put the plan into code. To keep this new methods small it is necessary to first create a slideLeft method and a slideRight method. Then incorporate them into the overall skate method.

Lesson 8.4 - Create a new method using a parameter

Now, to get real fancy and add a spin method to spin the skater in a realistic manner. The spin method will require a parameter to tell the skater how many times to spin.

1. Spin
   a. Parameter: How many times
   b. Do in order
      i. prepare to spin
         1. Do together
            a. move arms up
            b. raise and turn left leg
      ii. spin the skater (how many times)
      iii. finish the spin
         1. Do together
            a. move arms down
            b. lower and turn left leg

Now code this operation and a new instance of a class has been created with more functionality than the original class. It has all of the old attributes, methods and functions plus some new ones to make the skater more realistic. Now it is time to look at how these methods cam be passed on to new instances of this class.

Lesson 8.5 - Creating a new class

The skater has been given some new capabilities and they should be captured to use for other skaters. This involves creating a new class of object which should be called "realSkater". This is a two step process.

1. Rename the iceSkater. THIS IS THE MOST IMPORTANT STEP! Save the iceSkater object with a different name so it does not write the methods into

the original class. Right click on the name of the object in the object tree and select rename. Select rename from the popup and then enter "realSkater" in the box.

2. Save the new class. Right click on "realSkater" in the Object tree and select save object. In the save object popup select the folder/directory where the class is to be saved and then click the Save button.

The class is automatically named with the new name beginning with a capital letter and a file name extension of .a2c which stands for Alice 2 Class.

Now that a new class has been created, it can be used in a new world by selecting Import from the File menu. This will bring this new 3D action figure into the world with all of the added functionality.

If we want to move this new object to another copy of Alice it can be found in the Alice directory. Look in the required directory for a subdirectory named Gallery. You will find the .a2c file here and you can then copy it to another copy of Alice. You can build a Gallery of your own objects to use and share with others.

Lesson 8.6 - Character Builder

Note: This is available in the People Gallery in Alice Versions 2.2 and 2.3. It requires a parameter change in Version 2.4. (See Appendix A)

Not enough different people for your movie? The character builder is the answer. Yes, build your own character. Add to the characters methods and function. Then, just as we learned in this lesson, save it for use in other movies. Now the characters are not super graphics but they will give you lots of flexibility in characters for your movies. Where do you find this character builder? At the end of the People gallery you will find a "hebuilder" and a "shebuilder". These enable you to build a male or female for your movie.

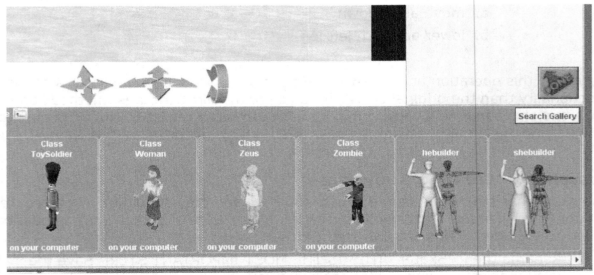

Figure 8.6.1

Add the instance to your movie, this may take a few seconds. They a dialog box will appear similar to Figure 8.6.2.

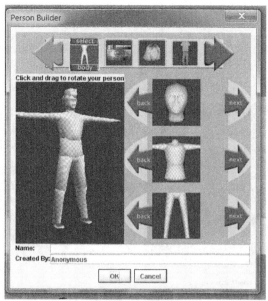

Figure 8.6.2

Let's examine this dialog box and start making changes. First, give your object a name and then give yourself some credit for this creation by putting your name in the Created by textbox.

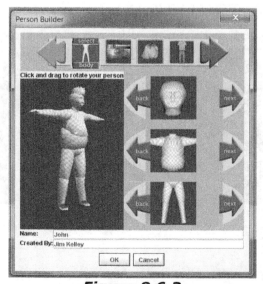

Figure 8.6.3

There is a group of selectors across the top. Body Changes, Face (upper -eyes, nose and lower – mouth), Hair Color and lastly change Shirt, Pants and Shoes. As you select options in these various selection areas, the image on the left will change accordingly. There are quite a few choices so getting it right may take some experimentation. I created John and came up with the person in Figure 8.6.4.

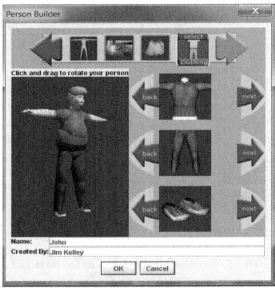

Figure 8.6.4

When you are satisfied with your person save the person to the world and get started on the new methods and functions to make your character truly your creation. Each person comes with inherited properties, methods and functions but get creative and make up some of your own.

Figure 8.6.5

As you can see from Figure 8.6.5 there are quite a choice of methods. Explore the properties, methods and functions before adding your own.

In Review

8.6.1 A "_____" and a "_____" class enable you to build a male or female object for your movie.

8.6.2 Each object you create from the character builder comes with _____ properties, methods and functions.

Lesson 8.7 - Try This

Now select an object and give it added functionality. Walk, turn the wheels, whatever will give a Class new functionality and realism. After creating the "new" class, don't forget to save it with a new name. If you forget this step you will change the old class and that is something that should be avoided. It is important to plan each new methods and to test them thoroughly before saving them to a new class.

Place several instances of this new object in a world and write a program to use this new functionality. Then import the new object into a new world to test the re usability of this new class. Remember, re usability is the key advantage of object oriented programming.

SECTION 2

This section contains some step-by-Step exercises to help the student understand the concepts presented in the first section. This section contains the following Step-by-Step exercises.

Step-by-Step 1 – The Step Sisters

Step-by-Step 2 - Billboard

Step-by-Step 3 – 3D Text

Step-by-Step 4 – Walk around the House

Step-by-Step 5 – Using Random Numbers

Step-by-Step 6 - Bi-Plane

Step-by-Step 7 - Penguin

Step-by-Step 8 – Spider JR

Step-by-Step 9 – Ice Skater

Step-by-Step 10 - Lost in Space

Step-by-Step 11 - Japan

Step-by-Step 12 - Animal Sounds

Step-by-Step 13 - Cowboy

Step-by-Step 14 - Follow the Car

Step-by-Step 15 - Dragon's Dance

Alice Exercise Topics

Answer Key for In Review Questions

Alice Step-By-Step 1

Exercise Uses:
- **Select a world**
- **Select Objects**
- **Single View / Quad View**
- **Methods**
  - **move up**
  - **move down**
  - **move forward**
  - **move backward**
  - **turn**
  - **say**

Open Alice and click on **Templates tab**.

Select **Grass World** and click **Open**

Click on **Add Objects** button (green button below grass).

Select **"People"** from the **Gallery**

Click on **"Class aliceLiddel"** and click on **"Add Instance to World"**

Click on **"Class evilStepsister1"** and click on **"Add Instance to World"**

Click on **"Class evilStepsister2"** and click on **"Add Instance to World"**

Click on the **quad view** radio button in the upper right corner of the screen. Use this view to line up all three objects.

Click on the **single view** radio button

Click on **"Done"** – green button screen far right.

Select **evilStepsister1** and under the **methods tab** select **evilStepsister1.say** and drag to the method editor. Click on **other** and Enter **"Alice, Jump!"**, click on **more..** and **duration 2 seconds**.

Select **aliceLiddel** and under the **methods tab** select **aliceLiddel.move** under the previous statement, select **UP** and **½ meter**.

Select **aliceLiddel**, drag the method **aliceLiddel.move** under the previous statement, select **DOWN** and **½ meter**.

Select **evilStepsister2** and under the methods tab select **evilStepsister2.say** and drag to the method editor. Click on **other** and Enter **"Alice, Turn!"**, click on **more..** and **duration 2 seconds**.

Select **aliceLiddel** and drag the method **aliceLiddel.turn** under the previous statement, select **RIGHT** and **1 revolution**.

Select **aliceLiddel** and drag the method **aliceLiddel.say** under the previous statement, select **goodby** and **duration 2 seconds**.

Select **aliceLiddel,** drag the method **aliceLiddel.move** under the previous statement, select **FORWARD** and **10 meters** then click on more... select **duration**, select **other**, click on the **3** and then click on **OKAY**.

PLAY the movie.

Alice Step-By-Step 2

Exercise Uses:
- **Select a world**
- **Select Make Billboard**

Open Alice and select a NEW **grass world**

From the Menu Bar, select **File** then the sub menu item **Make Billboard**

The Import dialog box will appear:

> Browse to jpg / gif / png graphic you wish to use for your billboard

> Click on **Import** Button

Click on **Add Objects** button.

Resize and adjust the image using the controls.

PLAY

Alice Step-By-Step 3

Exercise Uses:
- **Select a world**
- **Select Objects**
- **3D Text**
- **Methods**
  - turn
  - roll
  - resize

Open Alice and select a NEW **space world**

Click on **Add Objects** to display the object gallery.

Go to **3D TEXT** and click. A dialog box will appear:

    Replace "The quick brown fox." with "Lost in Space?"

    Change the Font to Comic Sans MS

    Click on the (B) Bold Button

    Click on the (I) Italics Button

Click on OK button.

Move your text up so it is displayed on the black sky.

Drag loop tile to the Methods Editor, set the loop to 5 times, do the following in the loop:

    Methods Tab: Set 3D Text.turn to left 1 revolution duration 2 seconds

    Methods Tab: Set 3D Text.roll to right 1 revolution

    Methods Tab: Set 3D Text.resize to ½ (half as big)

    Methods Tab: Set 3D Text.resize to 2 (twice as big)

PLAY

Alice Step-By-Step 4

Exercise Uses:
- Select a world
- Select Objects
- Single View / Quad View
- Do in Order
- Do Together
- Methods
  - move up
  - move down
  - move forward
  - move backward
  - turn
  - say

Open Alice and select a NEW **grass world**

Go to **Buildings** and put a **FARMHOUSE** on the world

Go to **People** and put a Class of **RandomGuy2** and a class of **Kelly** on the world.

Kelly may be over the RandomGuy2 so we need to:

move Kelly to the right.

move the Kelly back to the front door of the Farmhouse.

move the RandomGuy2 slightly to the left.

Click on DONE button.

Select Kelly in the object tree and place a command in the world event area to move her forward to stand next to RandomGuy2.

This may require some experimentation as to how many meters she will have to move

Have Kelly say "Do you want to go for a walk?"

Select RandomGuy2 in the object tree and have him respond "OK!"

Test your movie.

Insert the "Do in order" command above the first command in the world events window. Then move up the commands below the structure into the "Do in order" structure.

Insert some comments

above "Kelly move" insert comment "Move people into position"

above "Kelly say" insert comment "Couples conversation"

below "Kelly say" insert comment "Turn to walk"

Make RandomGuy2 turn right ¼ revolution

Make Kelly turn right ¼ revolution

TEST – not the girl is behind the boy and needs to be by his side to walk properly.

Move girl forward ½ meter BEFORE she makes the turn.

Move the girl forward to his side AFTER she makes the turn, this will require some experimentation.

Drop the "Do Together" after the turn to walk comment but before the "RadnomGuy2 turn right"

Drag the commands into the "Do Together" structure.

RandomGuy2 turn right

Kelly move

Kelly turn

Kelly move

TEST (note how this happens much smoother)

Create another "Do together" structure.

In the new structure place

RandomGuy2 turn right one revolution as seen by the Farmhouse (entire Farmhouse)

Kelly turn right one revolution as seen by the Farmhouse (entire Farmhouse)

TEST

Since this is too fast change the duration for both objects to a duration of 5 seconds.

TEST.

Save your project and name it WALK

Alice Step-By-Step 5

Exercise Uses:
- **Select a world**
- **Select Objects**
- **Single View / Quad View**
- **Variables**
- **Random Numbers**
- **Loop**
- **If/Else (Nested)**
- **Ask user for input**
- **Methods**
  - **move forward**
  - **move backward**
  - **turn**

This lesson uses Decisions, Repetition, and Random Numbers.

Open Alice and select the snow world

Go to the Animal Gallery and select the penguin object three (3) times.

Get all three penguins to face the camera.

Using Quad View make sure they all line up.

Generate the code to make each penguin move forward one meter and then move back one meter in a loop structure that has them perform the action two times.

Create a new numeric variable and name it selectPenguin and set value to 1

Drag it to the line above the first "Loop 2 times" and set value = 1.

Select the World Object and go to Functions and find the function that asks "ask the user for a number", drag and drop over the 1 in the variable command you created in step 7, then set the following question text "Which penguin would you like to move 0, 1, 2?"

Penguin1 = 0; Penguin2 = 1; Penguin3 = 2

Set up a "Nested If Statement.

Drag an If/Else statement up to the World Event Editor, drop right after the "Loop 2 times" statement and select "true".

Drag a second If Else statement to the "Else" side of the first If/Else statement, once again, select true.

Drag the Loop for Penguin to the true side of the first If statement.

Drag the Loop for Penguin1 to the true side of the second If statement.

Drag the Loop for Penguin2 after the Else in the second If statement.

Drag and Drop the selectPenguin variable to the true in the first If statement and replace it and change to == and value to 0.

Drag and Drop the selectPenguin variable to the true in the second If statement and replace it and change to == and value to 1.

PLAY

Now, let's change this movie to have the "Three Penguin Stooges" move forward and back randomly.

Delete or Disable the instruction that asks for a number.

Drag and Drop selectPenguin variable in the same place in the code set value = 1.

Set the World Object and select random number and drag to the variable instruction and drop over the 1

Select more and set minimum = 0.

Select more again and set maximum = 3. This is a glitch in the random number generation. You need to select a number 1 higher than the maximum number you will need.

Select more again and set "integer only" = true.

PLAY repeatedly to make sure all the penguins move.

Alice Step-By-Step 6

Exercise Uses:
- **Select a world**
- **Select Objects**
- **Events**
- **Create a New Method**
- **Create a New Event**
- **Single View / Quad View**
- **Methods**
  - **move up**
  - **move down**
  - **roll**
  - **move forward**
  - **turn**
  - **say**

Biplane Exercise (Events):

Open Alice and select the Sand World (for a change)

Select the BiPlane Object - position to screen right and it should be less than 10 percent of the width of the screen (move it back in the world)

Go to the methods tab in the details area

Click on "create new method"

NAME:flyForward

OK

       Drag Do Together to the Methods Editor

              biplane move forward 2 meters

Go to the methods tab in the details area

Click on "create new method"

NAME:roll

OK

       Drag Do Together to the Methods Editor

              biplane move forward 2 meters

              biplane roll left 1 revolution

Go to the methods tab in the details area

Click on "create new method"

NAME:flyUp

OK

Drag Do Together to the Methods Editor

      biplane move forward 5 meters

      biplane move up 5 meters

Go to the top right to the Events Editor Window

Click on "Create New Event"

Select "When a key is typed"

Click on "Any Key"

Select "left"

Click on "Nothing"

      Select biplane

      select method flyForward

Go to the top right to the Events Editor Window

Click on "Create New Event"

Select "When a key is typed"

Click on "Any Key"

Select "up"

Click on "Nothing"

      Select biplane

      select method flyUp

Go to the top right to the Events Editor Window

Click on "Create New Event"

Select "When a key is typed"

Click on "Any Key"

Select "space"

Click on "Nothing"

      Select biplane

      select method roll

PLAY

ALICE Step-By-Step 7

Exercise Uses:
- **Select a world**
- **Select Objects**
- **Change properties**
- **Proximity Functions**
- **Single View / Quad View**
- **Methods**
  - move up
  - move down
  - walk
  - move backward
  - turn to face

PROBLEM: A penguin turns to face a hole in the ice, regardless of where the hole is located. The penguin should then walk to the center of the hole and jump into it, disappearing below the surface of the ice.

PSEUDOCODE:

> penguin turns to face the hole
>
> penguin walks distance to the center of the hole
>
> penguin falls down into the hole

STEPS:

Create a Snow World

Add a penguin from the animals gallery

Add a Hole (circle) from the Shapes gallery

Change the color property to blue. (details panel)

Select the penguin object

Drag & Drop tile for "turn to face" method into the Methods Editor.

Select turn towards the circle object

penguin turn to face circle more...

Penguin class has a custom method named "walking"

Walking x (set x = 1)

Replace the 1 set in the prior step with a call to the "penguin distance to" function.

Use the functions tab in the details panel

Look in the proximity category

Make sure you select the circle object

penguin walking x = penguin distance to circle

To make penguin fall into the hole

move penguin down until he is below the ice (approx. 5 meters).

penguin move down 5 meters more...

Code in Methods Editor should look like this:

penguin turn to face circle more...

penguin walking x = penguin distance to circle

penguin move down 5 meters more...

Test your movie, make any necessary changes.

Can you improve this movie? Example: make a fish jump out of the hole and back in to entice the Penguin to move to the hole.

Alice Step-by-Step 8

Exercise Uses:
- **Select a world**
- **Select Objects**
- **Change properties**
- **Proximity Functions**
- **Single View / Quad View**
- **Methods**
  - ○ **move toward**
  - ○ **move down**
  - ○ **move forward**

This exercise creates a movie where a spider object moves to a space ship object. The code moves parts of the legs in the proper sequence to simulate life-like movement of the legs.

Spider Jr.

- Line up Spider and Lunar lander as shown in picture 1

- Picture 2 shows the result

- Using the code provided, recreate this scene.

- The spider moves towards the lunar lander, I looped 8 times, you may have to adjust this for your spacing of the two objects.

- You may need to experiment some but this simulates leg movement.

This is the code for Spider Jr.

world.my first method ( )
No variables

spiderRobot turn to face lunarLander
Loop 8 times times
Do together
spiderRobot move amount = 1 meter **toward** target = **lunarLander** duration = 0.5 seconds style = **abruptly**
Do in order
spiderRobot.body.backLeftLegBase.upperJoint turn forward .1 revolutions duration = 0.5 seconds
spiderRobot.body.backLeftLegBase.upperJoint turn backward 0.1 revolutions duration = 0.5 seconds
Do in order
spiderRobot.body.frontRightLegBase.upperJoint turn forward 0.1 revolutions duration = 0.5 seconds
spiderRobot.body.frontRightLegBase.upperJoint turn backward 0.1 revolutions duration = 0.5 seconds
Do in order
spiderRobot.body.frontRightLegBase.upperJoint turn backward 0.1 revolutions duration = 0.5 seconds
spiderRobot.body.frontRightLegBase.upperJoint turn forward 0.1 revolutions duration = 0.5 seconds
Do in order
spiderRobot.body.backRightLegBase.upperJoint turn backward 0.1 revolutions
spiderRobot.body.backRightLegBase.upperJoint turn forward 0.1 revolutions
spiderRobot say Momma! duration = 2 seconds

Run the movie. Carefully observe the leg movement. Can you improve the action?

Alice Step-by-Step 9

Exercise Uses:
- **Select a world**
- **Select Objects**
- **Create a new Class**
- **Create new methods**
- **Single View / Quad View**
- **Methods**
  - **turn**
  - **move**

The Ice Skater

This exercise requires a snow world with the ice lake and the ice skater loaded. This illustrates how we can create new classes of objects after giving them new methods.

Complete the following exercise and at the end see how to create a new class that can be used in other exercises.

After she skates across the ice we will execute a spin method which more closely simulates an ice skater spinning. Enter the following code to complete the movie. Note how the spin now includes the arms and legs with a more life-like motion.

IceSkateWorld's Code

Created by: Jim Kelley

world

Events

111

When the world starts

Do:

world.my first method

Methods

world.my first method ( )
No variables

   Loop 5 times **times**

      iceSkater.skate

   iceSkater.spin howManySpins = **2**

   Loop 2 times **times**

      iceSkater.skate

iceSkater

Methods

iceSkater.slideLeft ( )
No variables

   Do in order

      Do together

         iceSkater.rightLeg turn forward .1 revolutions duration = **0.5** seconds

         iceSkater.upperBody turn forward 0.01 revolutions duration = **0.5** seconds

      Wait 0.5 seconds

      Do together

         iceSkater.rightLeg turn backward 0.1 revolutions duration = **0.5** seconds

         iceSkater.upperBody turn backward 0.01 revolutions duration = **0.5** seconds

iceSkater.slideRight ( )
No variables

   Do in order

      Do together

         iceSkater.leftLeg turn forward 0.1 revolutions duration = **0.5** seconds

         iceSkater.upperBody turn forward 0.01 revolutions duration = **0.5** seconds

      Wait 0.5 seconds

      Do together

iceSkater.leftLeg turn backward 0.1 revolutions duration = **0.5** seconds

iceSkater.upperBody turn backward 0.01 revolutions duration = **0.5** seconds

iceSkater.skate ( )
No variables

Do together

iceSkater move forward 2 meters duration = **3** seconds

Do in order

iceSkater.slideLeft

iceSkater.slideRight

iceSkater.prepareToSpin ( )
No variables

Do together

iceSkater.upperBody.chest.leftShoulder.arm turn backward 0.5 revolutions

iceSkater.upperBody.chest.rightShoulder.arm turn backward 0.5 revolutions

iceSkater.leftLeg turn left 0.2 revolutions

iceSkater.leftLeg turn backward 0.25 revolutions

iceSkater.finishSpin ( )
No variables

Do together

iceSkater.upperBody.chest.leftShoulder.arm turn forward 0.5 revolutions

iceSkater.upperBody.chest.rightShoulder.arm turn forward 0.5 revolutions

iceSkater.leftLeg turn right 0.2 revolutions

iceSkater.leftLeg turn forward 0.25 revolutions

iceSkater.spin ([123] **howManySpins**)
No variables

Do in order

iceSkater.prepareToSpin

iceSkater turn left howManySpins revolutions

iceSkater.finishSpin

Now let's rename this skater "fancyIceSkater" and save as a new object to be used later. Click on iceSkater in the Object tree and select rename. Rename the object then right click again and save the new class in an appropriate directory.

Can you add the proximity function to this movie?

Alice Step-By-Step 10

Exercise Uses:
- **Select a world**
- **Select Objects**
- **Single View / Quad View**
- **3D Text**
- **Move Camera**
- **Change Properties**

Open Alice and click on **Templates tab**.

Select **Space World** and click **Open**

From the SPACE Gallery select:

      Astronaut

      LunarLander

Position them on the screen

Go to their properties and set them both:

      isShowing = False

Then, back to the Gallery and go to the 3D Text Selection and place on the screen.

Select:

      Lucinda Console

      Bold

      Italics

      Text = Lost in Space

      Properties of 3D Text: Change color to Orange

In the code

    Wait 10 Seconds

    Set the properties of the 3D Text: isShowing = False

    Do Together

            Astronaut: property: isShowing = True

            LunarLander: property: isShowing = True

    Move Camera back 10 meters.

○ world.my first method

world.my first method *No parameters*

No variables

```
Wait  10 seconds

3D Text   set isShowing to   false   more...

Do together
    lunarLander   set isShowing to   true   more...
    astronaut   set isShowing to   true   more...

camera   move  backward   10 meters   more...
```

Alice Step-By-Step 11

Exercise Uses:
- **Select a world**
- **Select Objects**
- **Single View / Quad View**
- **3D Text**
- **Change Properties**
- **Methods**
  - ○ **move camera**

Open Alice and click on **Templates tab**.

Select Sand World and click Open

Go to Japan Gallery and Select:

    dojo

    Two samauri

    One fandancer

Using the left, right, forward, back Arrows (arrow group on the left):

Scroll left to the outside of the dojo to the sand world.

    Place and position the Temple Object from the Gallery

Using the arrows again, go back to inside the dojo.

Select 3D Text object and make the following property changes:

    Text = JAPAN

    color = red

    isShowing = False

Code:

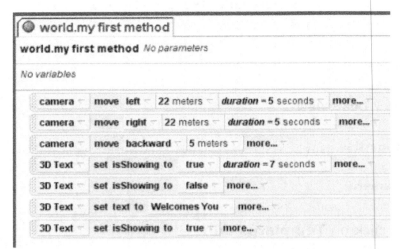

Outside the dojo:

Back inside the 3D Text appears:

Then a second message appears:

Alice Step-By-Step 12

Exercise Uses:
- **Select a world**
- **Select Objects**
- **Single View / Quad View**
- **Methods**
  - **move**
  - **play sound**

Open Alice and click on **Templates tab**.

Select Grass World and click Open

From the Animal Gallery Select:

> lion
>
> monkey
>
> mouse
>
> husky
>
> cat
>
> bird1
>
> cow

All of these objects have built in sound. Now we will create code to let them display their golden voices.

Code:

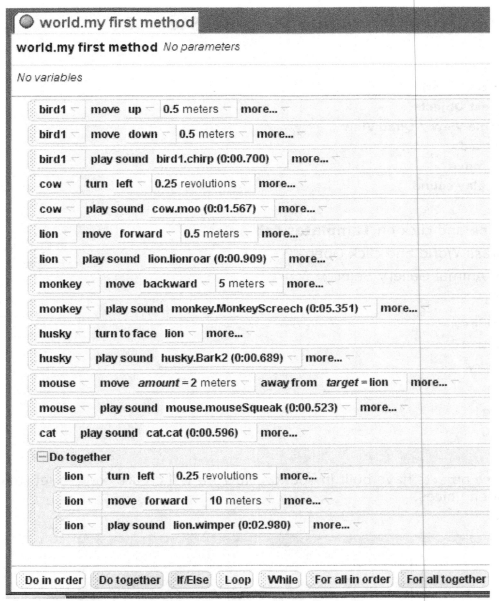

world.my first method

world.my first method *No parameters*

No variables

| bird1 | move up | 0.5 meters | more... |

| bird1 | move down | 0.5 meters | more... |

| bird1 | play sound bird1.chirp (0:00.700) | more... |

| cow | turn left | 0.25 revolutions | more... |

| cow | play sound cow.moo (0:01.567) | more... |

| lion | move forward | 0.5 meters | more... |

| lion | play sound lion.lionroar (0:00.909) | more... |

| monkey | move backward | 5 meters | more... |

| monkey | play sound monkey.MonkeyScreech (0:05.351) | more... |

| husky | turn to face lion | more... |

| husky | play sound husky.Bark2 (0:00.689) | more... |

| mouse | move *amount* = 2 meters | away from *target* = lion | more... |

| mouse | play sound mouse.mouseSqueak (0:00.523) | more... |

| cat | play sound cat.cat (0:00.596) | more... |

⊟Do together

| lion | turn left | 0.25 revolutions | more... |

| lion | move forward | 10 meters | more... |

| lion | play sound lion.wimper (0:02.980) | more... |

Do in order   Do together   If/Else   Loop   While   For all in order   For all together

Now Play the concert.

Alice Step-By-Step 13

Exercise Uses:
- **Select a world**
- **Select Objects**
- **Single View / Quad View**
- **Methods**
  - **play sound**
  - **turn**

Open Alice and click on **Templates tab**.

Select Sand World and click Open

From the Old West Gallery Select:

> Saloon

> Cowboy

You will need your favorite cowboy song in an .mp3 format. The cowboy will sing your song and move his arms. The movement is not very sophisticated but you can improve on this as you improve your Alice skills

CODE:

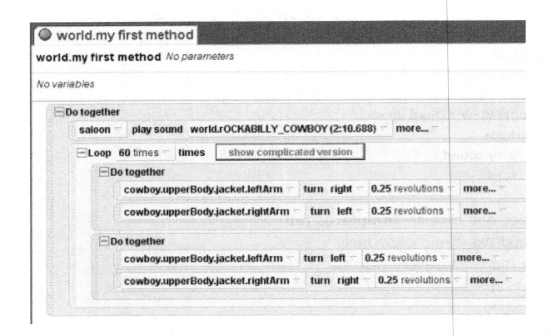

You will need to coordinate the timing and duration of the cowboy's movements to go with the length of the song. This is perhaps the most difficult part of creating the movie. Note that in the code, the duration of the movie is displayed.

Alice Step-By-Step 14

Exercise Uses:
- **Select a world**
- **Select Objects**
- **Single View / Quad View**
- **Methods**
  - **move**
  - **turm**

Open Alice and click on **Templates tab**.

Select Grass World and click Open

From the City Gallery Select:

        BuildingCluster1

        BuildingCluster2

        BuildingCluster3

        BuildingCluster4

        BuildingCluster5

        Church

From the Vehicles Gallery Select:

        Any car, I selected the StationWagon for my movie.

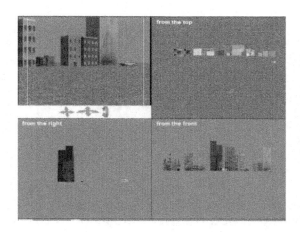

Arrange the BuildingCluster1 – 5 in a row with the Church object at the end. They need to be in a straight line so you will need the quad view to line them up properly. My example moves the car from right to left so I put the car at the right end of the line of buildings and adjusted the camera manually.   Now, experiment to move the car along the fronts of the buildings moving the camera to keep the movement in the playing screen. This takes some experimentation to make the whole movie run smoothly. I had to back up the camera as it panned the line of buildings and adjust the speed to keep the car in the movie screen.

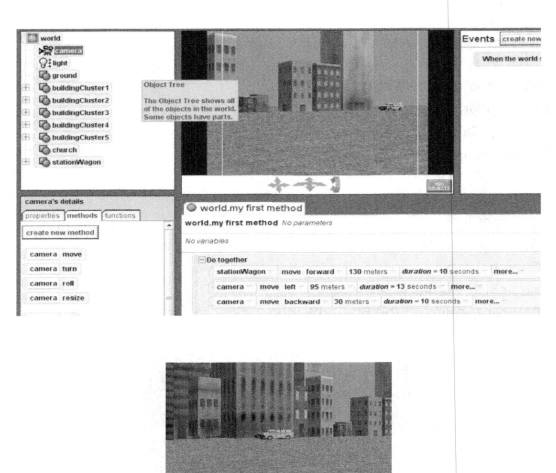

After you master this you can add the city landscape with streets, lights, etc. to make it more realistic. It is useful just to play with something simple like this to learn how camera movement and object movement need to be coordinated.

Alice Step-By-Step 15

Exercise Uses:

- **Select a world**
- **Select Objects**
- **List**
- **For All in Order**
- **For All Together**
- **Single View / Quad View**
- **Methods**
  - move
  - turn

Open Alice and click on **Templates tab**.

Select Grass World and click Open

From the Fantasy Gallery Select:

    3 copies of the Dragon object.

Use Quad View to place the dragons in a line.

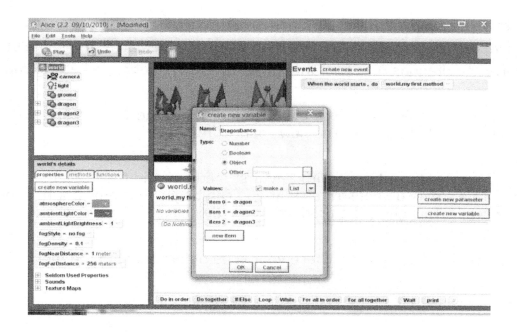

In the Object Tree Select the World Object.

Under properties select "New Variable"

      Name: DragonDance

      Check "make a" and select LIST from the dropdown.

      Add each dragon to the list

      Click on OK

Select tab for World Methods

Click on "Create New Method"

      Name the new method "dance"

Drag For all in Order to the methods editor.

      Select expression...

      Select world.Dragon.Dance

      Drag the item_from_DragonDance down to the "Do Nothing"

      Select turn left 1 revolution.

This makes the dragons turn around one revolution, one at a time

Now, have the Dragons move backward 5 meters, one at a time.

The next two steps use the For all Together tile.

      Have the dragons move up and then down 1 meter, all at the same time.

      Have the dragons turn forward one complete revolution, all at the same time.

No drag the new method up to the event editor "When the World starts do" to replace "My First Method" with the new "dance" method.

Most of our movies have begun with "My first method" and then called other methods. This movie demonstrates that you can begin your movie with another method as well. This gives the producer more flexibility in running the movie.

See the code example below to check your code before running the movie.

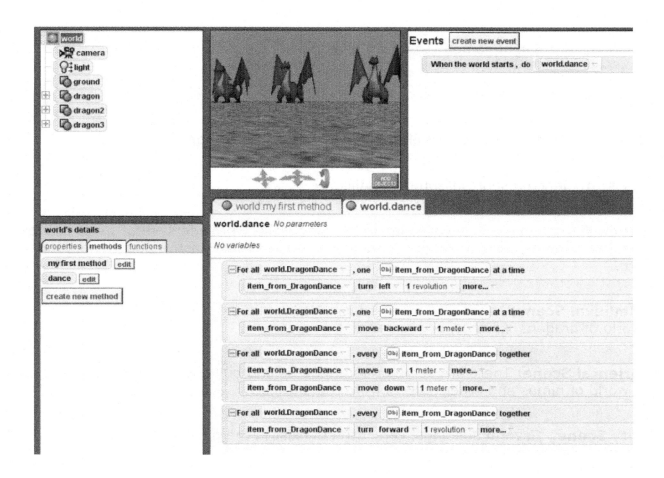

PLAY the Movie and when it starts, the dance should begin.

OTHER IDEAS FOR PROJECTS

Alice Exercise Topics

If you can't think of something for an Alice movie, here are some ideas:

Favorite Movie: Create a scene from your favorite movie.

How To: Using Alice objects illustrate how to do something.

Lesson: Teach a short lesson using Alice.

Moon World: The Space collection in the Web Gallery provide several space related classes. Create your own moon world with a moon surface, astronauts, lunar lander, etc.

Medieval Scene: In the Gallery there is a Medieval Collection of classes. Create a world of dragons, knights, princesses and castles.

Oriental Scene: There are some oriental figures and buildings. Use them to create a world of ninjas and other objects from the far east.

City Scene. Several buildings, cars, streets exist in the gallery. Use these to create a city street scene.

Airport Scene: Use the airport buildings, runways and airplanes to build a airport.

School Scene: There are a lot of school objects in Alice 2.2. Use them to create a scene at school or in the gym.

Underwater World: create an underwater world of fishes and scuba divers.

Arctic World: Create a snow world with classes that is filled with classes appropriate for this venue.

Holiday Scene: There are a number of holiday objects, create a scene for your favorite holiday.

WORD PROBLEMS FOR ADDITIONAL EXERCISES

Exercise 1:

Create an Alice world where a person is in a rowboat yelling "Help!" while two sharks circle the boat. Be sure to make the sharks circle the boat at the same time. Also, be sure to change some of the default settings to control how fast the sharks swim around the boat.

Exercise 2:

Create a world that contains any object that contains a turn method. When the world first begins, ask the user for the number of times they want the object to spin. If that number is less than 10, then use the turn method to spin the object that number of times. If the number is 10 or more, the object should say "Spinning more than 10 times makes me sick!".

Exercise 3:

Create an amusement park that has several rides. Activate those rides to spin or turn and have a number of people objects and other amusement activities in the scene. Let the mouse move the camera to show the entire park from different perspectives. Use the billboard object to create signs around the park.

Exercise 4:

Create a sea world with an island and a fish. The fish should swim around the island. (Part of the fish's body should be above the water's surface, so you can see it swimming.) The program should ask the user for the number of fish from 1 to 6 and that many fish should swim around the island ten (10) times.

Exercise 5:

Create a world with an instance of the Lake Class (from the environments collection) and an instance of the IceSkater class (from the people collection). Program the IceSkater so she skates around in a circle on the lake. When the program starts it should ask the user how many times she should circle the lake and if she should jump each time she finishes a loop. The skater should circle the number of times entered and jump at the end of each circle.

Exercise 6:

Create your own story that includes the following elements:

   ask the user for at least one input.

   has at least one variable.

   multiple objects move together.

   changes a property value of one or more objects.

   User interaction with the mouse, or arrow keys.

Exercise 7:

Alice Version 2.4 includes the "Garfield" characters. Using these characters bring your favorite Garfield cartoon to life. Make a Garfield movie using one of the many Garfield cartoons or create your own cartoon.

Exercise 8:

Pick your favorite Alice movie and make a video from that project. Then upload your movie to YouTube and view your creation on the Internet.

ANSWER KEY FOR IN REVIEW QUESTIONS

Chapter 1 – Alice Basics

QUESTION	ANSWER
1.0.1	Method Editor
1.0.2	Properties, Methods, Functions
1.0.3	World View Window
1.0.4	True
1.0.5	Events
1.1.1	Four
1.1.2	Help, Tutorials
1.1.3	False
1.2.1	Properties, Methods, Functions
1.2.2	Methods
1.2.3	Properties
1.2.4	recipe
1.2.5	object, objects, objects
1.4.1	top, front, side
1.4.2	scroll view, zoom
1.4.3	layout
1.4.4	seven
1.5.1	storyboard
1.5.2	script
1.5.3	True
1.5.4	planning
1.6.1	outline
1.6.2	programming another language.
1.6.3	storyboarding, pseudocode

Chapter 2 – Alice Programming

QUESTION	ANSWER
2.0.1	front, back, left, right, top, bottom
2.0.2	methods
2.0.3	six degrees of freedom
2.0.4	False
2.1.5	details
2.1.1	quad
2.1.2	center
2.1.3	up, down
2.1.4	forward, backward
2.1.5	right, left
2.2.1	primitive
2.2.2	right click, object tree
2.3.1	variable
2.3.2	true
2.3.3	four
2.3.4	number, boolean, object, other
2.4.1	mouse
2.4.2	syntax
2.4.3	function
2.4.4	world object
2.4.5	string
2.5.1	Do Together
2.5.2	specific order
2.5.3	Do Together
2.5.4	Do in order

Chapter 3 - Decisions

QUESTION	ANSWER
3.1.1	logical
3.1.2	relational

3.1.3	three
3.1.4	six
3.1.5	boolean
3.2.1	billboard
3.2.2	GIF
3.2.3	PNG
3.2.4	file, Make Billboard
3.3.1	two
3.3.2	true
3.3.3	false
3.4.1	.MOV
3.4.2	Export Video
3.5.1	html
3.5.2	Desktop

Chapter 4 - Repetition

QUESTION	ANSWER
4.0.1	simple, complex
4.0.2	two
4.0.3	repetition
4.0.4	infinite
4.0.5	false
4.1.1	loop
4.1.2	variable
4.1.3	negative number
4.3.1	while
4.3.2	pretest
4.3.3	true
4.5.1	World Object
4.5.2	False
4.5.3	True

4.5.4	random number
4.6.1	list
4.6.2	For all in order
4.6.3	For all together
4.7.1	array
4.7.2	element
4.7.3	asterisk (*)
4.7.4	false
4.7.5	array

Chapter 5 - Methods

QUESTION	ANSWER
5.0.1	methods
5.0.2	penguin
5.1.1	class level methods
5.1.2	class, method
5.1.3	true
5.4.1	parameter
5.4.2	argument
5.5.1	World View
5.5.2	properties, methods, functions

Chapter 6 – Functions

QUESTION	ANSWER
6.0.1	function
6.0.2	method
6.0.3	return
6.1.1	world
6.1.2	user
6.2.1	center-point, center-point
6.2.2	functions

6.3.1	value
6.3.2	parameter
6.4.1	dummy objects
6.4.2	move to

Chapter 7 - Events

QUESTION	ANSWER
7.0.1	events
7.0.2	world.myfirstmethod
7.0.3	interaction
7.0.4	Create New Event
7.1.1	mouse
	keyboard
	events that occur during program execution.
7.1.2	Create New Event
7.1.3	When the world starts
7.2.1	When a variable changes
7.2.2	When the world starts
7.2.3	While something is true
7.3.1	When a key is typed
7.3.2	Let the arrow keys move <subject>
7.4.1	Let the Mouse move <object>
7.4.2	Let the mouse move the camera
7.5.1	sound
7.5.2	by looking at the dialog box when creating the object
7.5.3	two
7.5.4	.wav, .mp3
7.6.1	one

Chapter 8 - Classes

QUESTION	ANSWER
8.0.1	class
8.0.2	classes
8.0.3	plus sign
8.0.4	class
8.1.1	new class
8.1.2	inherit
8.1.3	properties, methods, functions
8.2.1	other objects
8.2.2	properties, methods, functions
8.2.3	True
8.6.1	hebuilder, shebuilder
8.6.2	inherited

Appendix A – HeBuilder / SheBuilder Change

This change applies to Alice Version 2.4

1. Go to the **File** Menu
2. Choose **Preferences**
3. Click on the **Seldom Used** Tab
4. Check **"he/she builder in gallery"**

Appendix B - Glossary of Terms

arguments	data elements passed to functions (often called parameters)
array	A set of indexed variables, all of the same data type.
boolean	evaluates to either of two conditions – True or False – Yes or No – 0 or 1
camelCase	in instances where spaces are not allowed, use camelCase to seperate words. First word starts with lower case subsequent words begin with upper case.
class	A collection of related properties, methods and functions that are a receipe for creating instances of objects.
Class-level variables	Variables that are available to all instances of a class of objects.
collate	to sort or put a list of items in order.
decision structure	Allows the program to evaluate an expression and take one path if true or a second path if false.
details panel	Shows detailed information about an object that has been selected in the World View window or in the Object Tree.
dialog box	A popup box that allows the programmer or user to select several related choices.
elements	each cell in an array is referred to as an element of the array
encapsulation	hiding the details of a method from the user
event	Events happen during the running of the Alice Movie. Start, Mouse movements, Key press, variables change, etc.
events editor	A list of events that are controlled by programs as the world plays
function	similar to a method only they return a value
inheritance	A collection of related properties, methods and functions that are a receipe for creating instances of objects.
instantiation	The act of adding an instance of a class of objects to the World View Window
list	An ordered set of data
local variables	Variables accessable only to the current running program code.
logical operators	Operators used to create a True/False (boolean) condition.
method	things an object can do.
methods editor	this is where you develop your code for your Alice project.
object	A group of properties that are all related and methods that can manipulate the object.
object tree	the upper left corner of the Alice environment that lists all of the objects on the stage.
opacity	the property that controls the degree of transparency of an object. Measured in percentages with 100% as the solid object and 0% as invisible.
orientation	the direction the front of an object is facing.
pan	moving the camera left or right without changing its position.
parameter variables	variables used to pass data to a function.
parameters	data elements passed to functions (often called arguments)
Pre-test loop	Evaluates the expression before entering the loop. Loop instructions may never be executed.
Post-test loop	Evaluates the expression at the end of the loop. Loop instructions are always executed once.
property	describes an object
quad view	an Alice selection that allows you to see front, top and side views
relational operators	evaluates two expressions and returns true or false
repetition structure	also referred to as the looping structure, a structure that repeats instructions until a condition is satisfied.
sequence structure	A group of instructions that are all executed in order without decision or repetition structures in the sequence.
six degrees of freedom	a 3D object has a front, back, top, bottom, left side, right side.
storyboarding	A group of pictures that ouline the story line of the movie.
string	zero or more alphanumeric characters
syntax	The rules for constructing the program statements.
toolbar	At the top of the Alice window that has several icons like Play, Undo, Trash, etc.
variable	A named memory location to hold values for use by the Alice program(s).
world view window	Shows a view of the virtual world. Has a camera object and a lighting object that may be manipulated to enhance the movie.
World-level variables	Variables available to all programs or objects that are part of the current Alice world.

Appendix C - Gallery of Classes
Version 2.4.1b

Amusement Park

Ancients

Animals

     Bugs

     Dinosaurs

Beach

Buildings

City

Controls

Egypt

Environments

     Skies

Fantasy

     Faeries

Farm

Furniture

Garfield

Hawaii

     Animals

     Environment

     People

     Plants

     Transportation

High School

     Students and Teachers

Holidays

Japan

Kitchen

       Food

Lights

Math

       Random Numbers

Medieval

Musical Instruments

Nature

Objects

Ocean

Old West

Park

People

Pilgrims

Planets

Roads and Signs

Science

SciFi

Shapes

State Park

Space

Special Effects

Sports

Vehicles

Visualizations

Create 3D Text

Appendix D - Gallery of Classes
Version 2.3

Amusement Park

Ancients

Animals

    Bugs

    Dinosaurs

Beach

Buildings

City

Controls

Egypt

Environments

    Skies

Fantasy

    Faeries

Farm

Furniture

Hawaii

Hawaii

    Animals

    Environment

    People

    Plants

    Transportation

High School

    Students and Teachers

Holidays

Japan

Kitchen

    Food

Lights

Math

Medieval

Musical Instruments

Nature

Objects

Ocean

Old West

Park

People

People

    Urban

    Walking People

Pilgrims

Roads and Signs

SciFi

Shapes

State Park

Space

Special Effects

Spooky

Sports

Vehicles

Visualizations

Create 3D Text

CPSIA information can be obtained at www.ICGtesting.com
Printed in the USA
LVOW03s1147150315

430620LV00013B/336/P